Forest Coloring Book For Adults

An Adult Coloring Book of 40 Woodland Designs and Wild Aniamls by a Variety of Artists

ISBN-13: 978-1523237920
ISBN-10: 1523237929

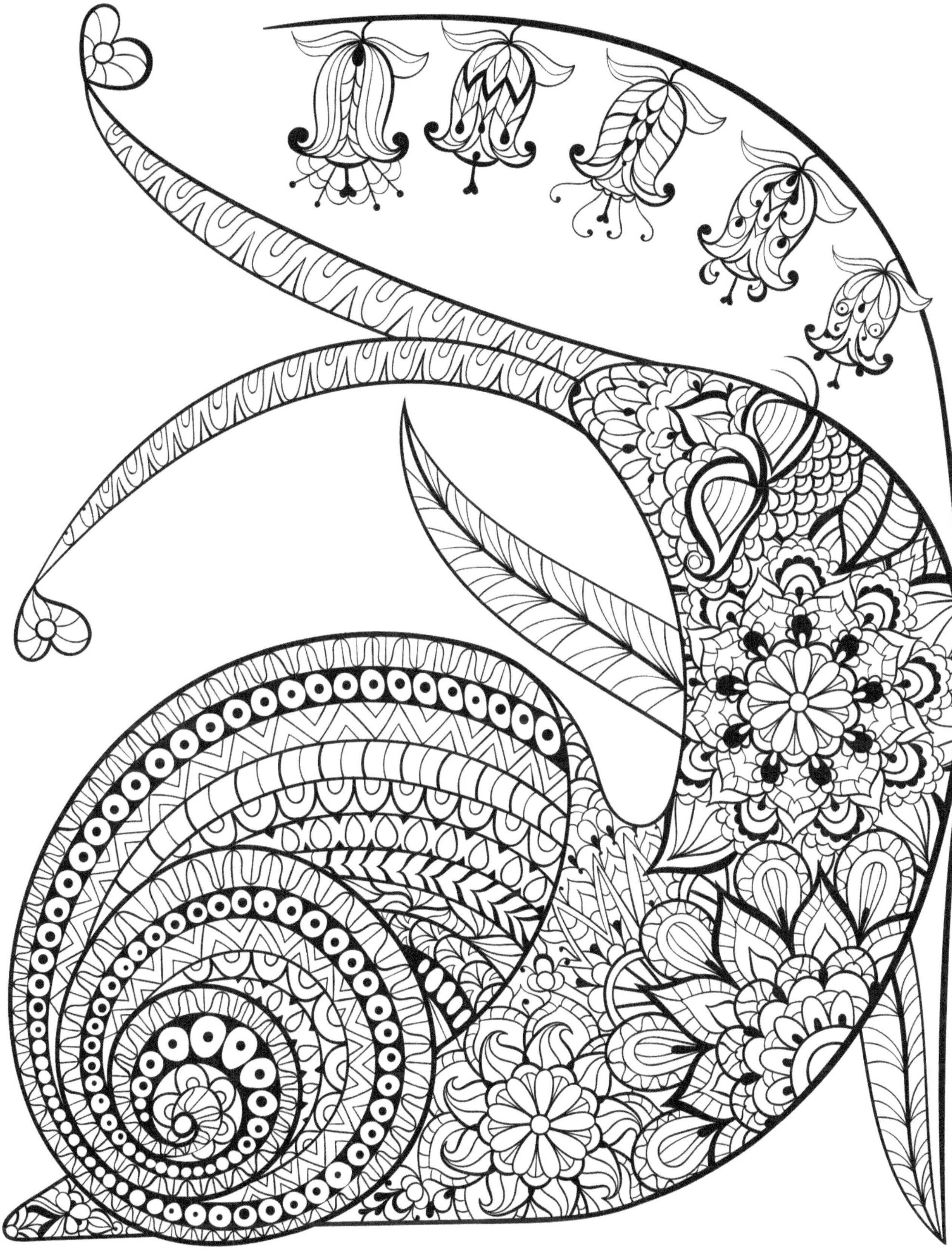

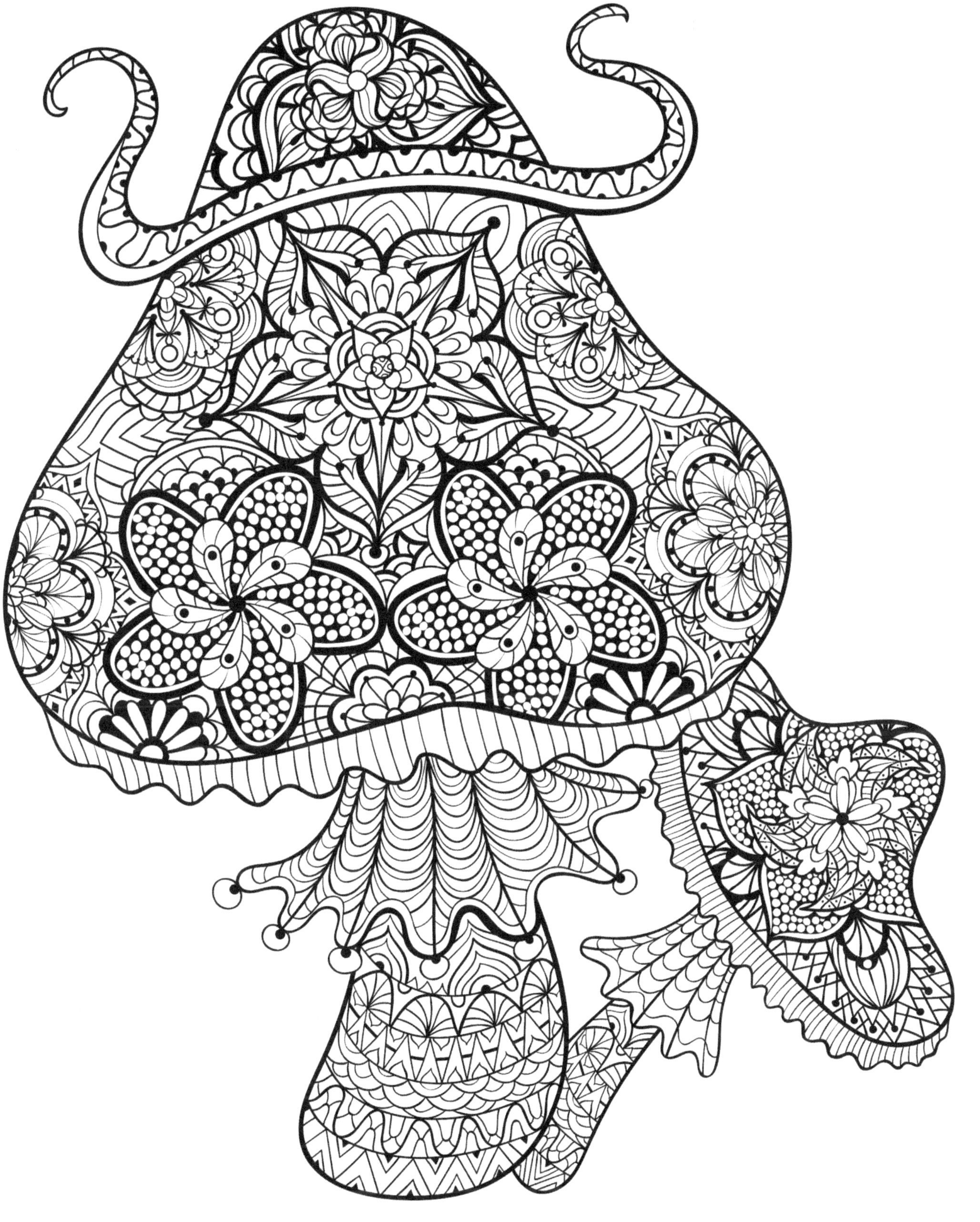

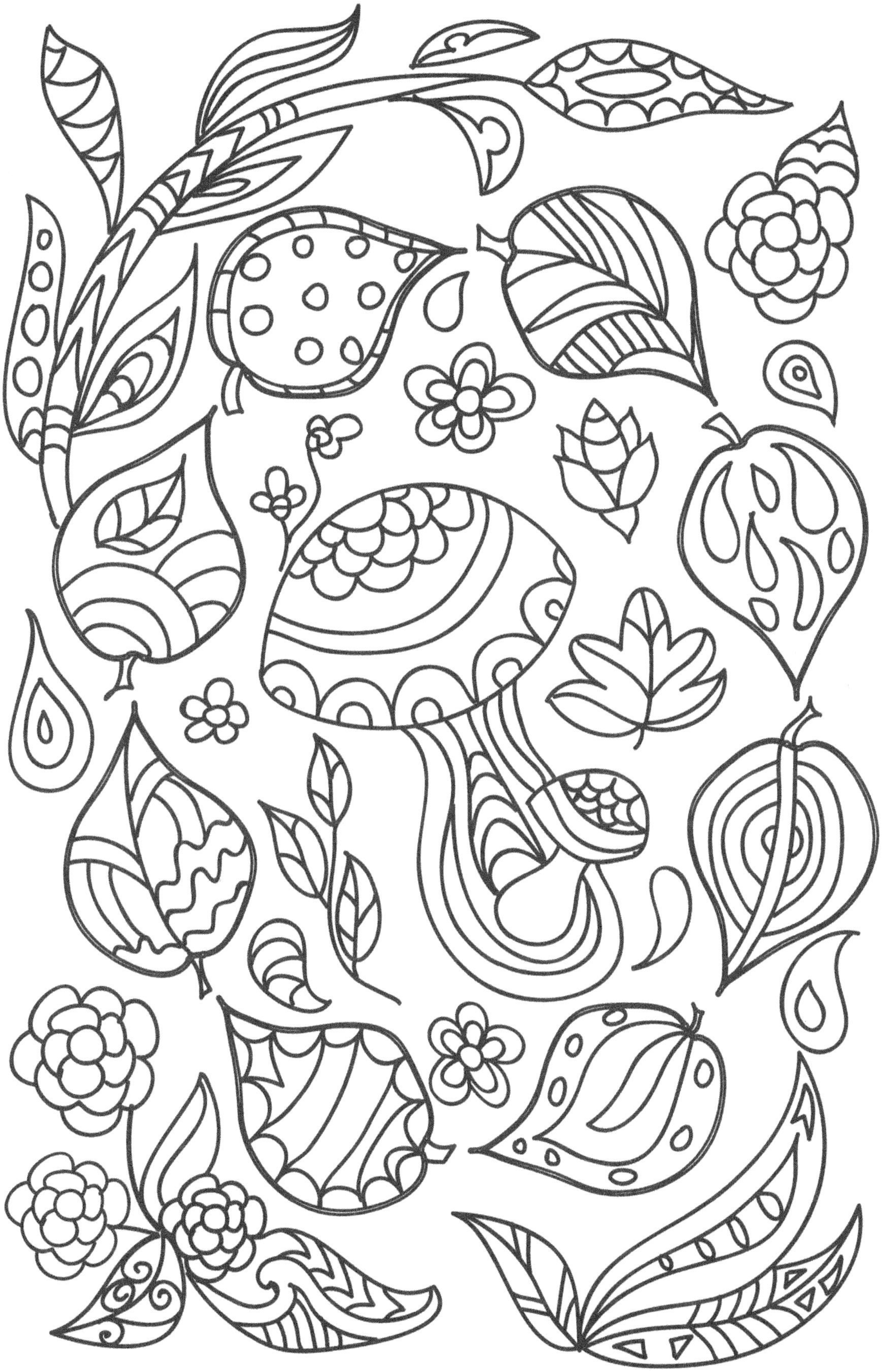

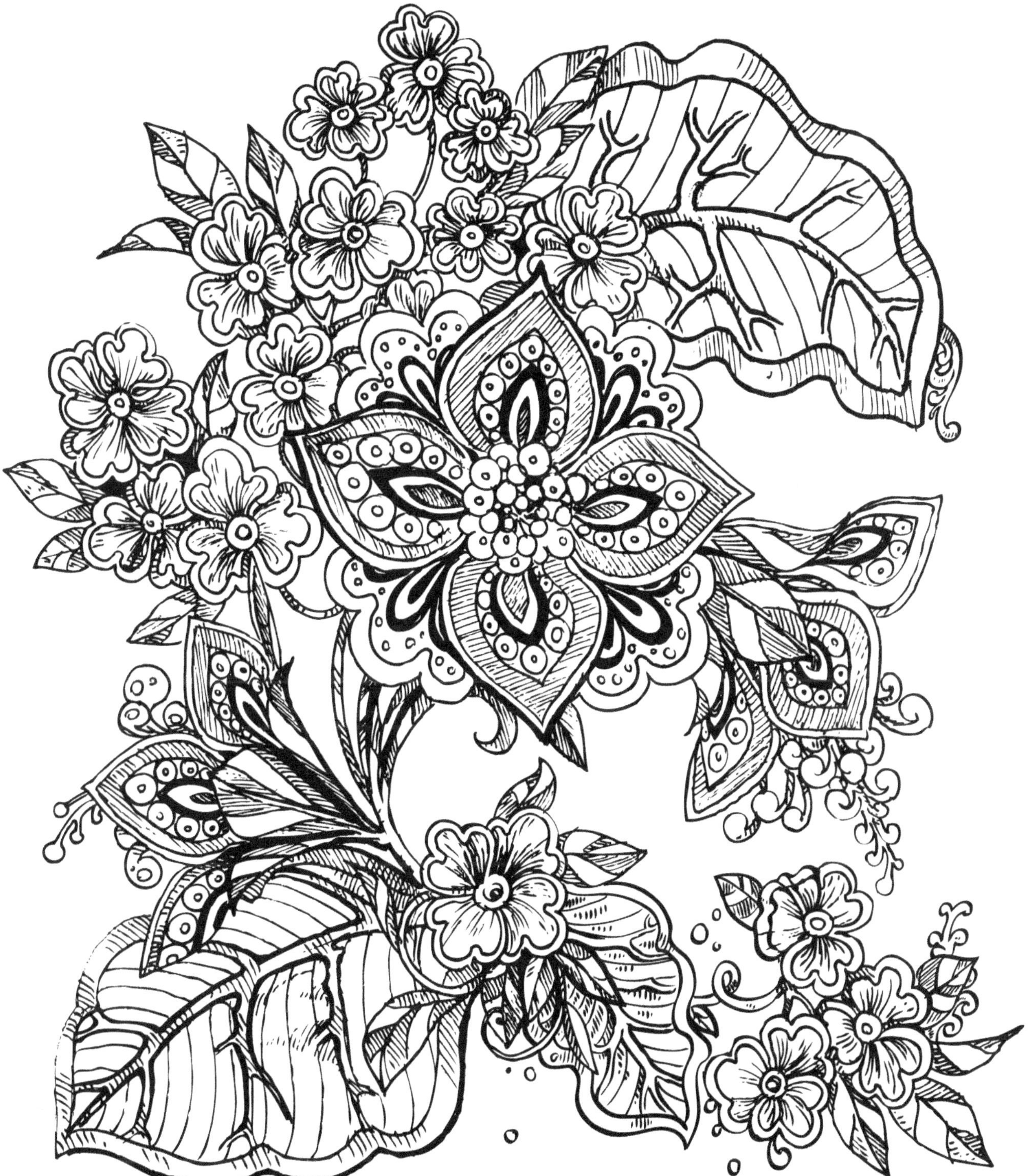

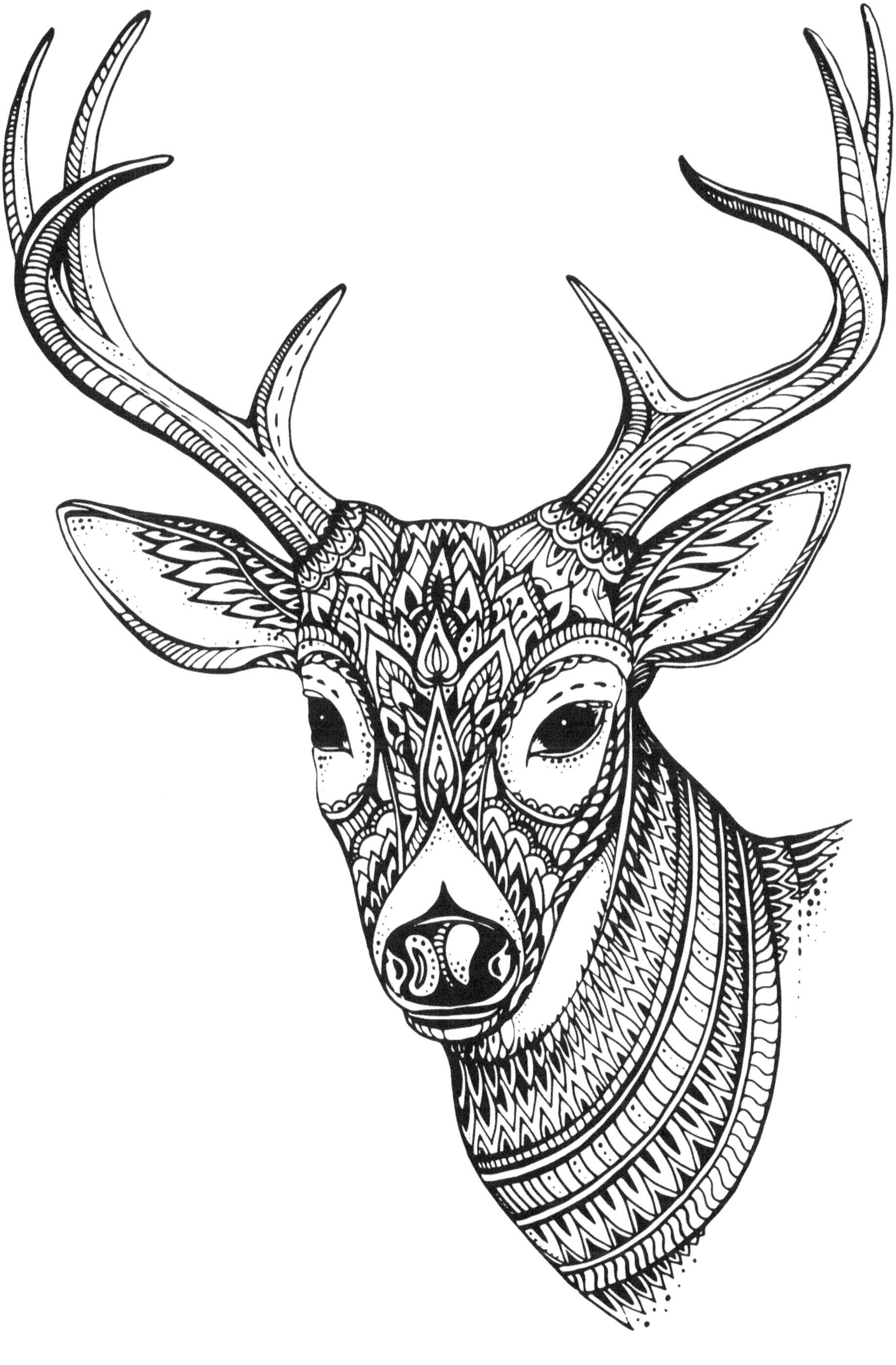

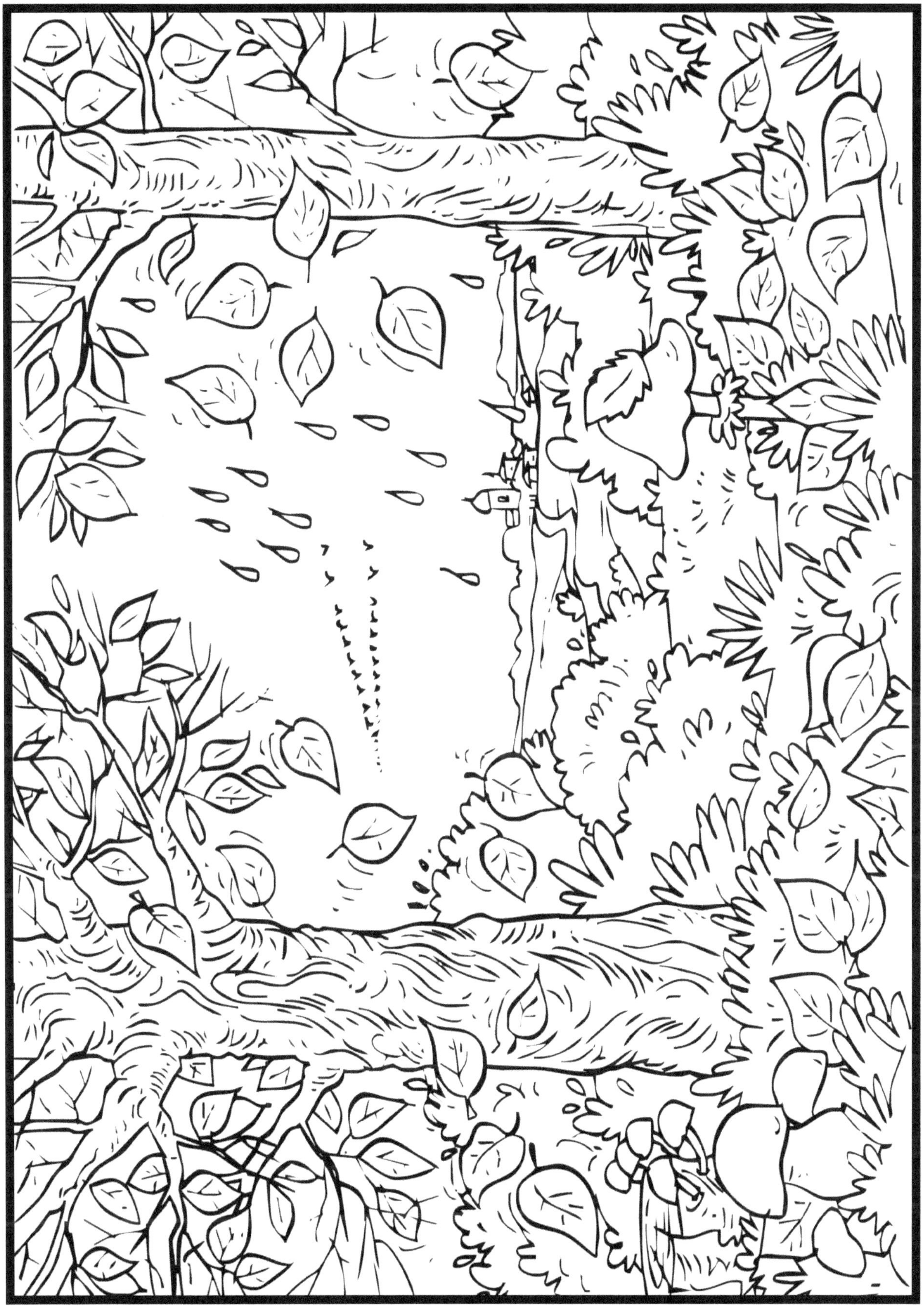

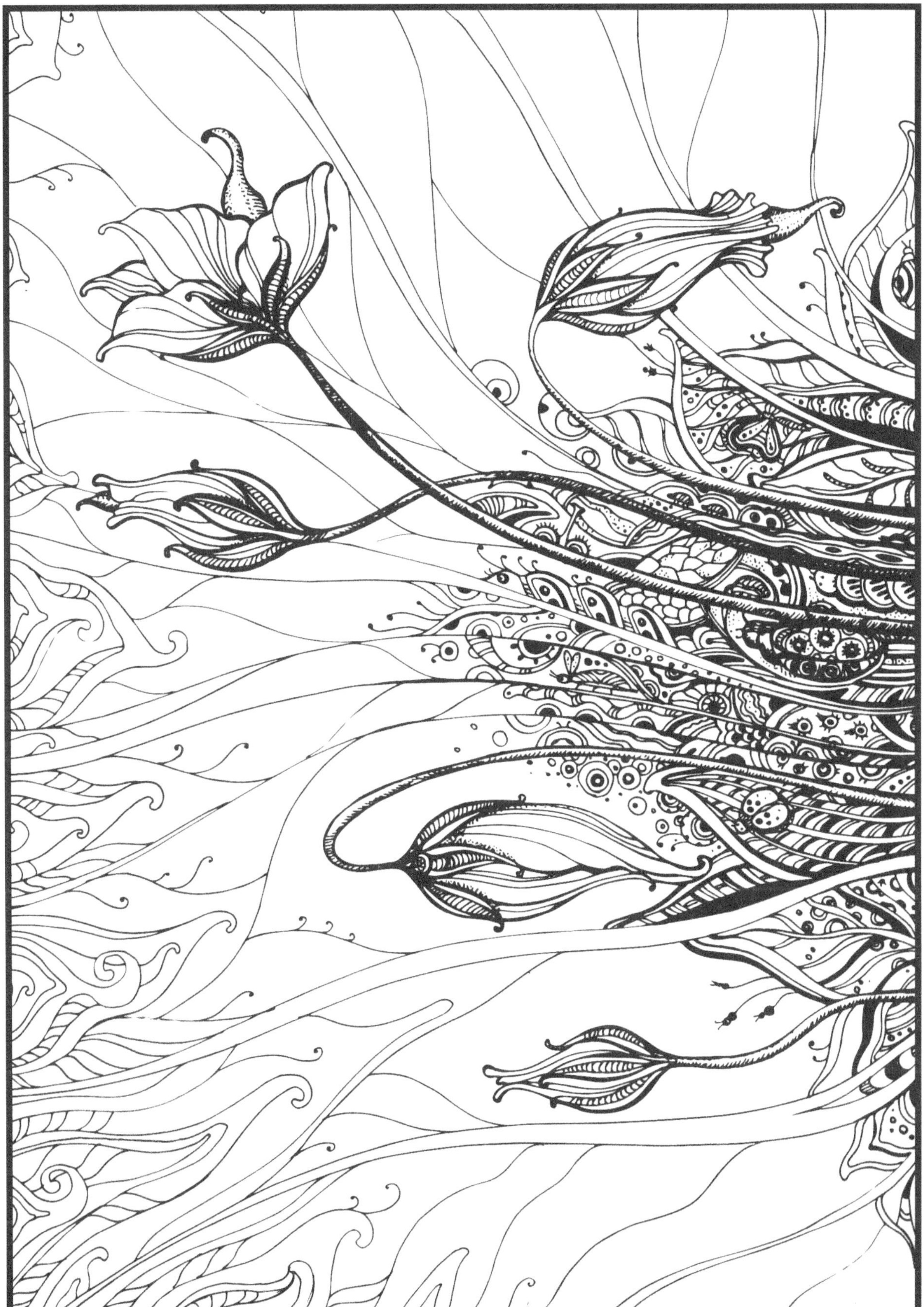

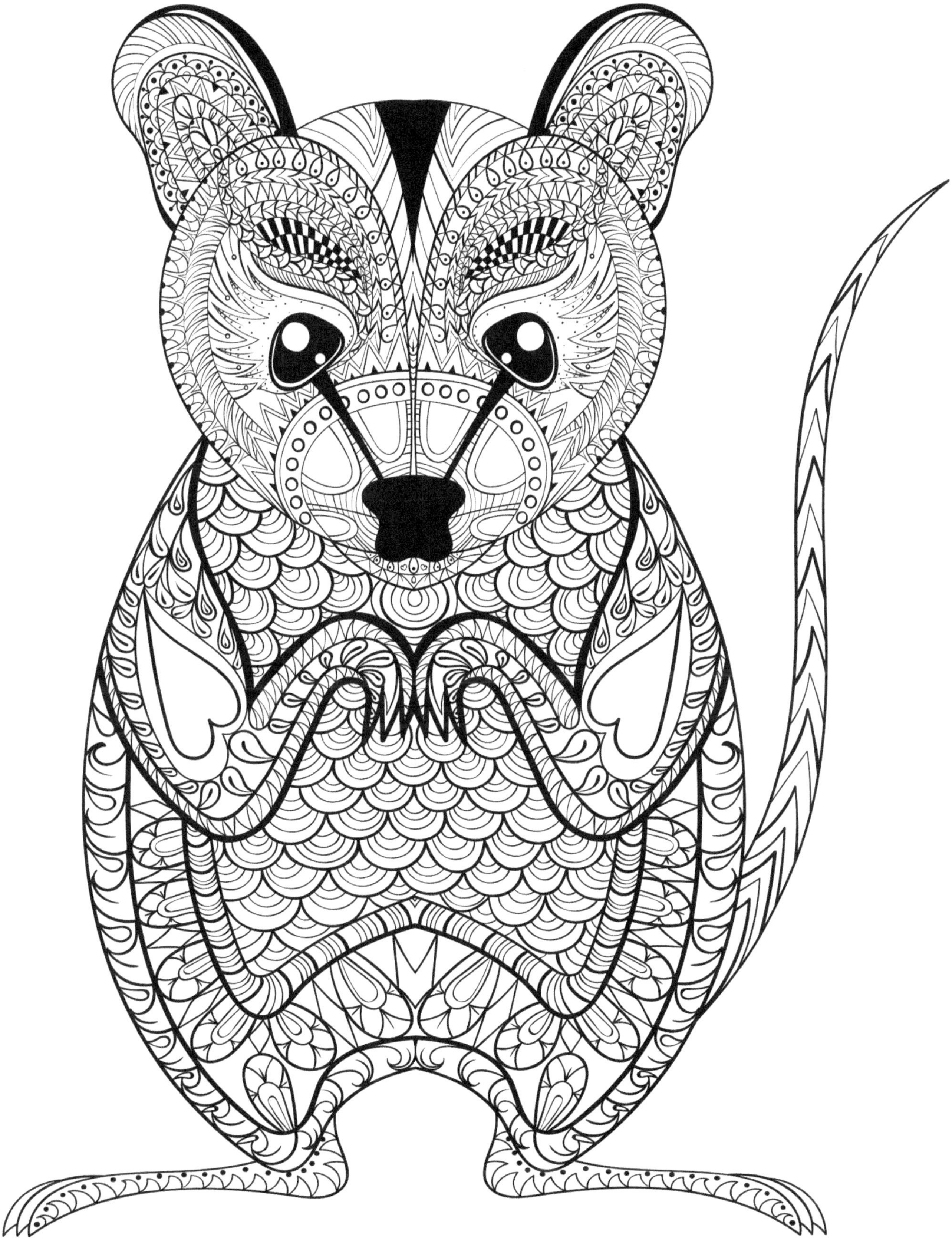

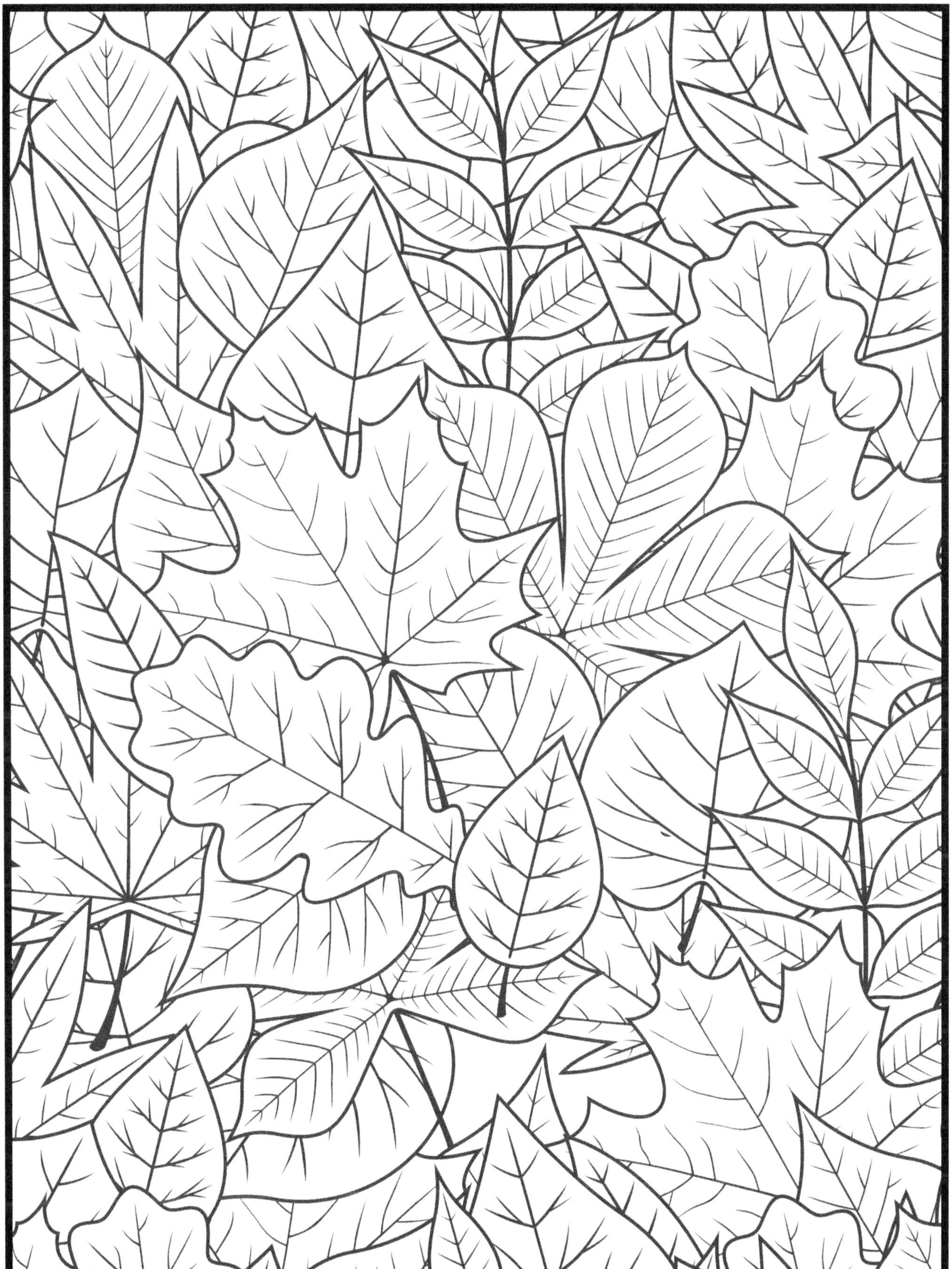

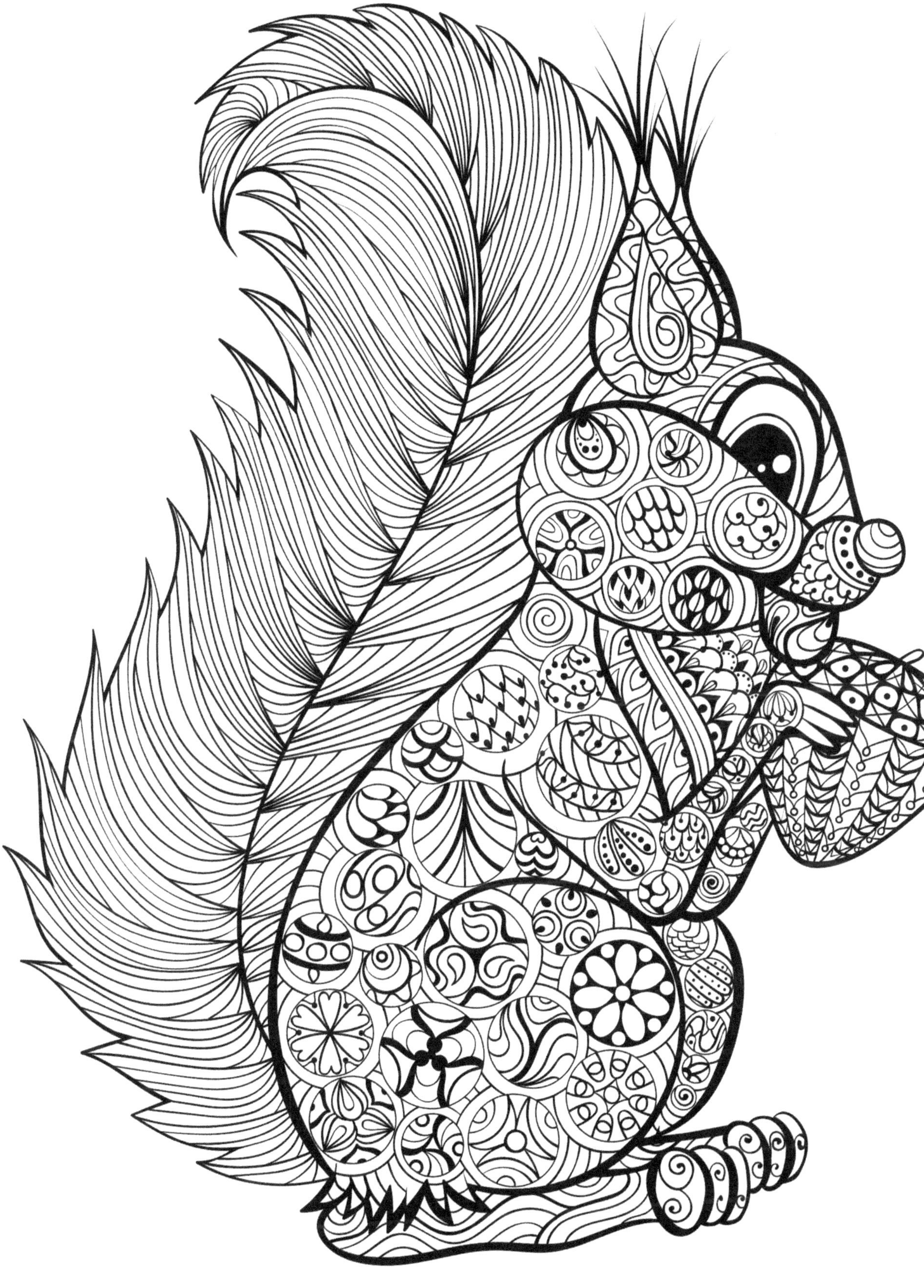

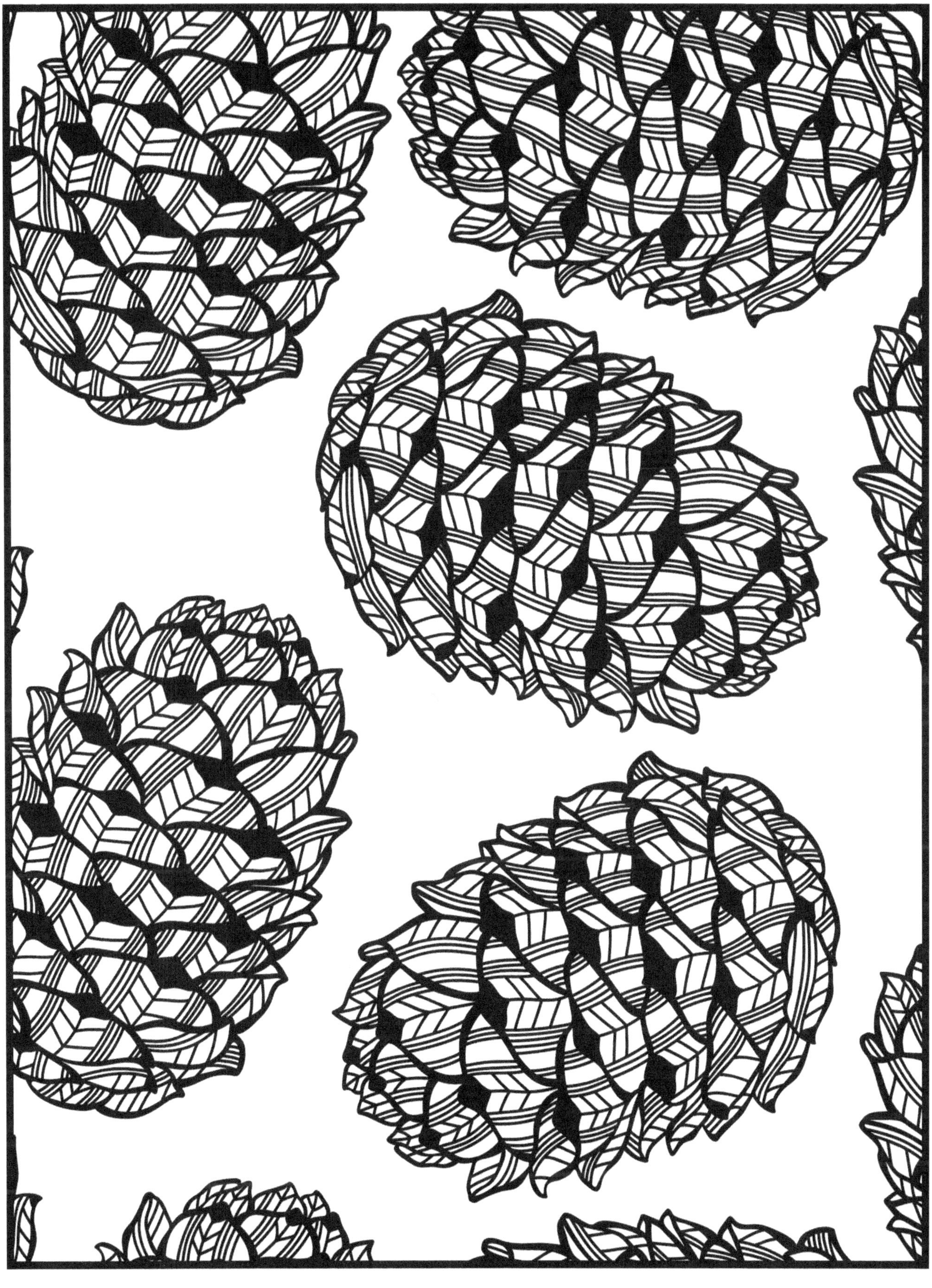

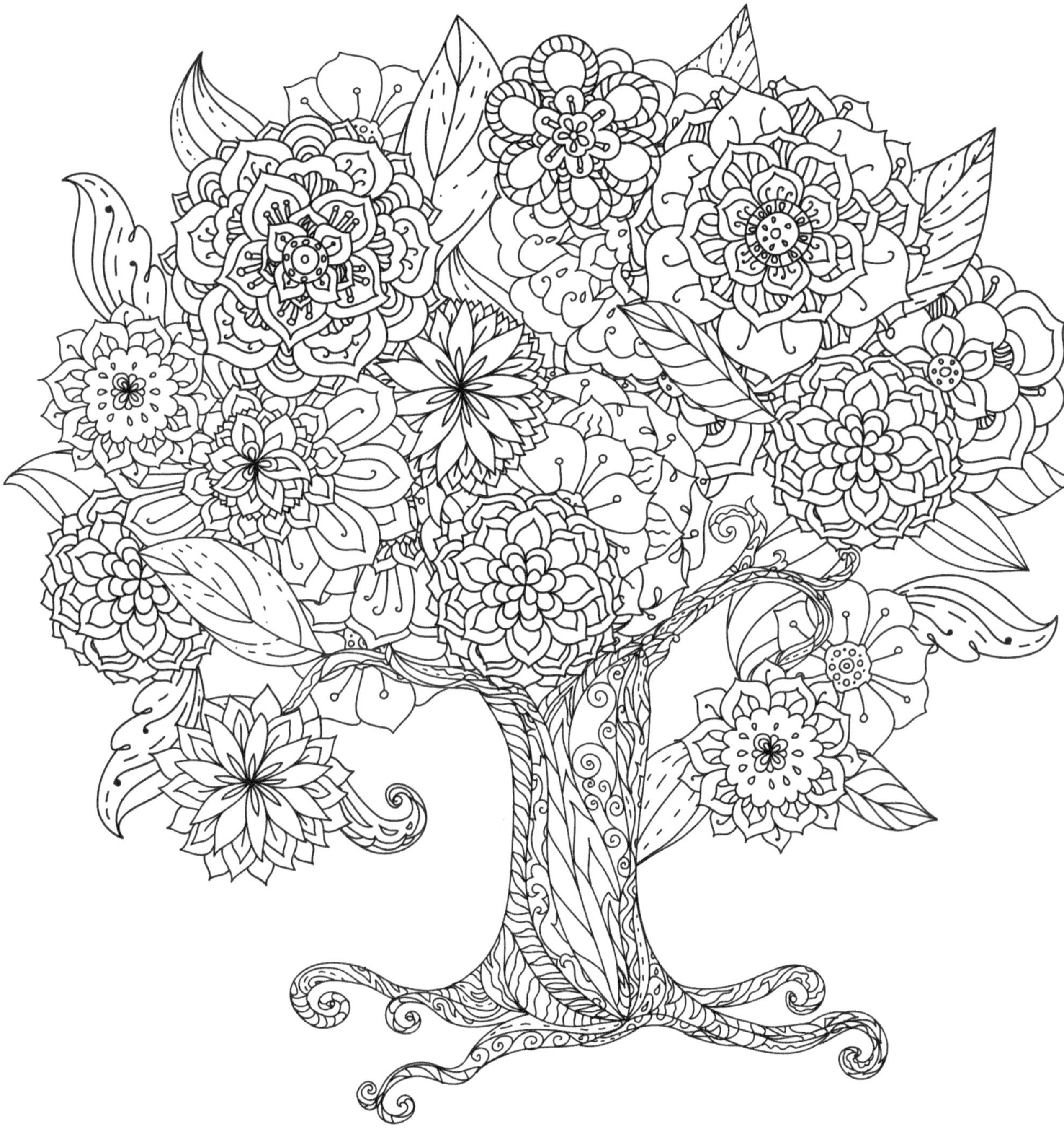

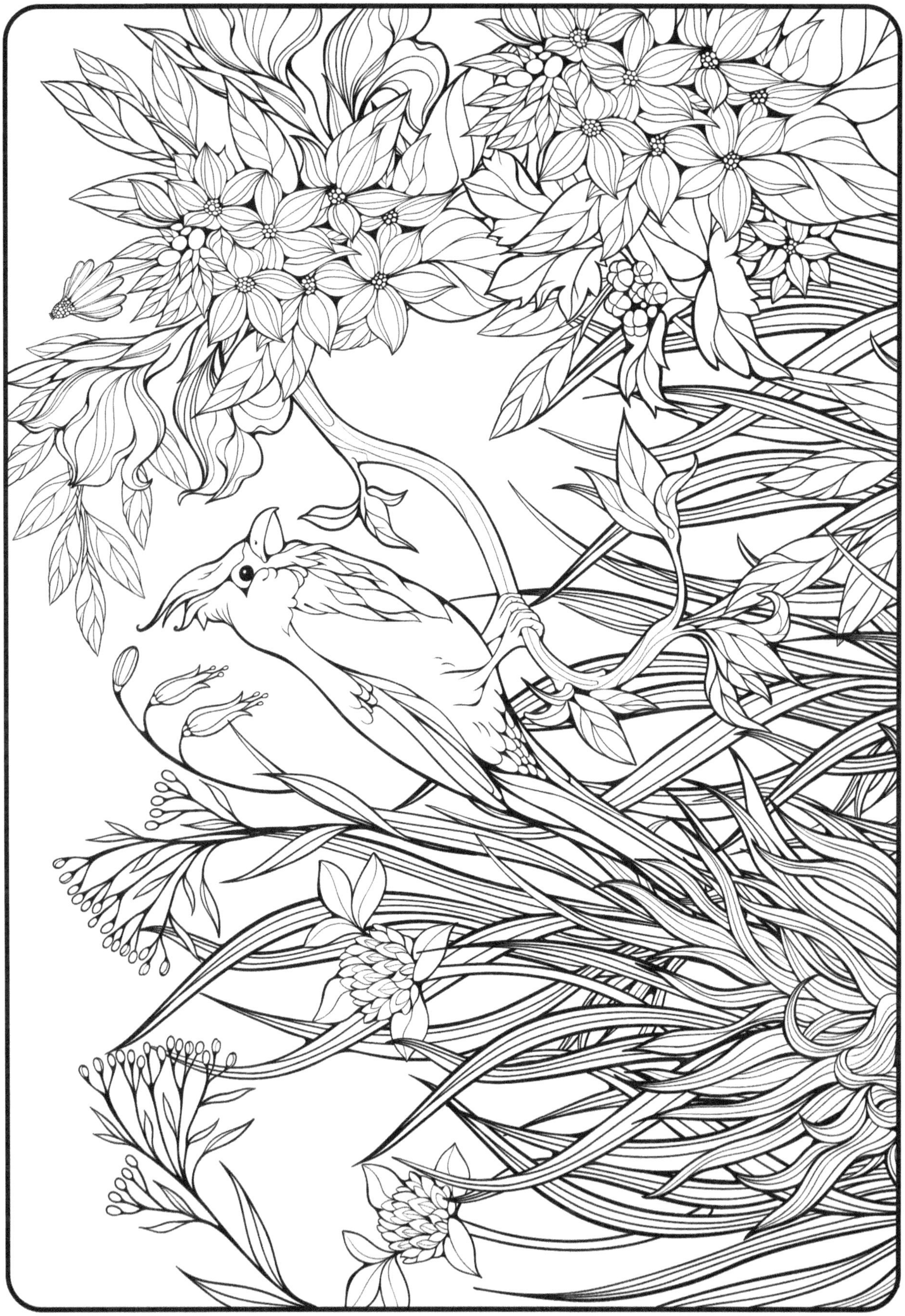

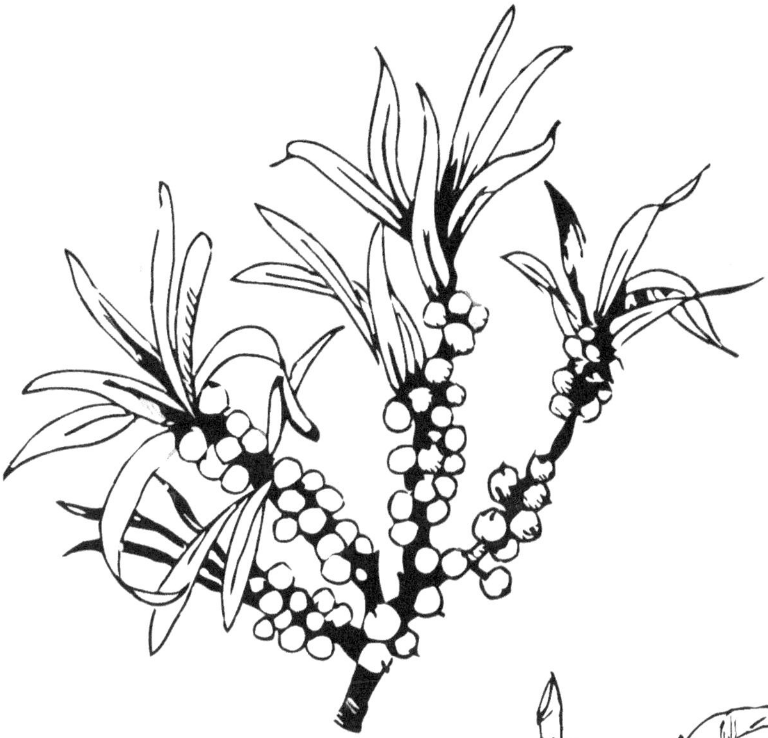
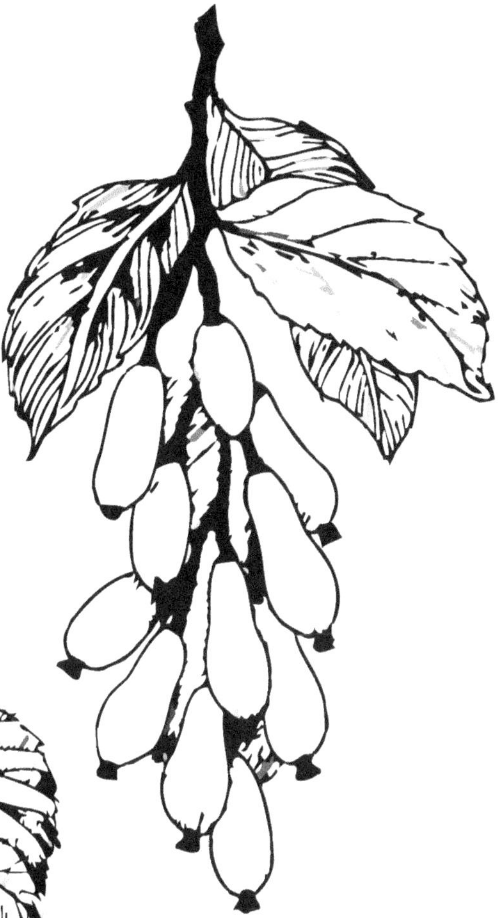
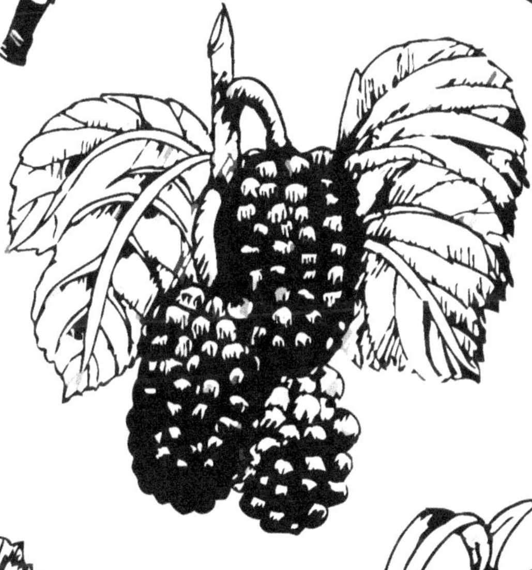
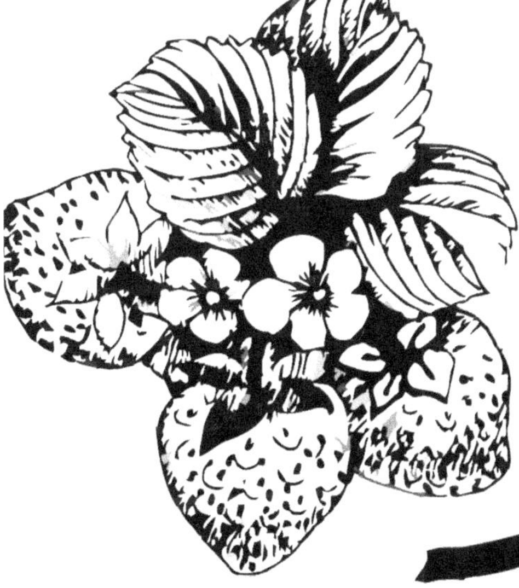
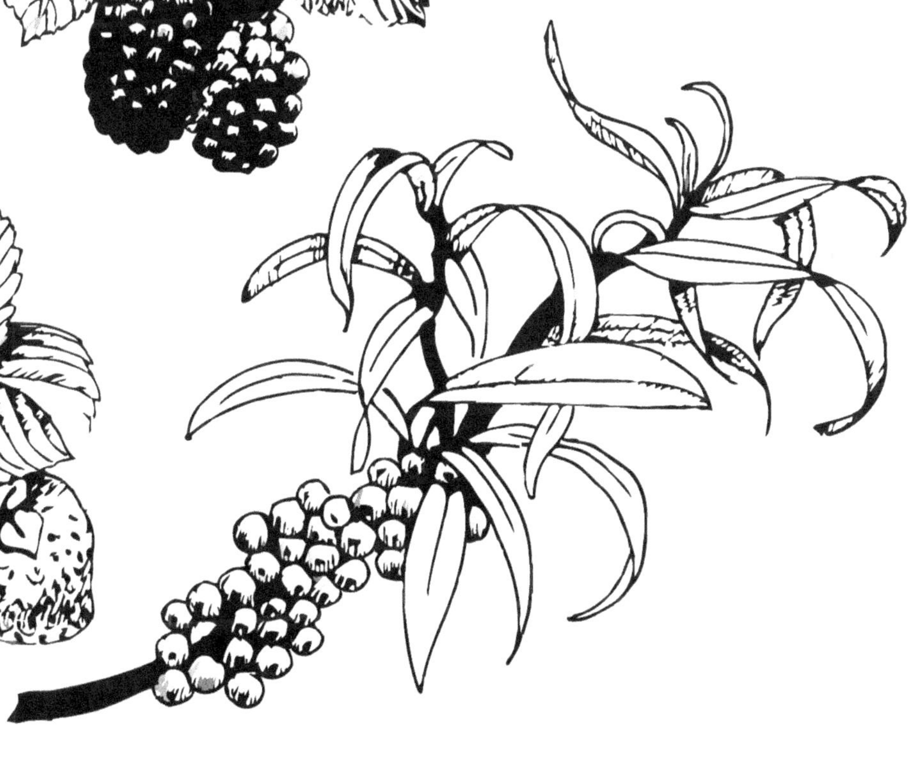

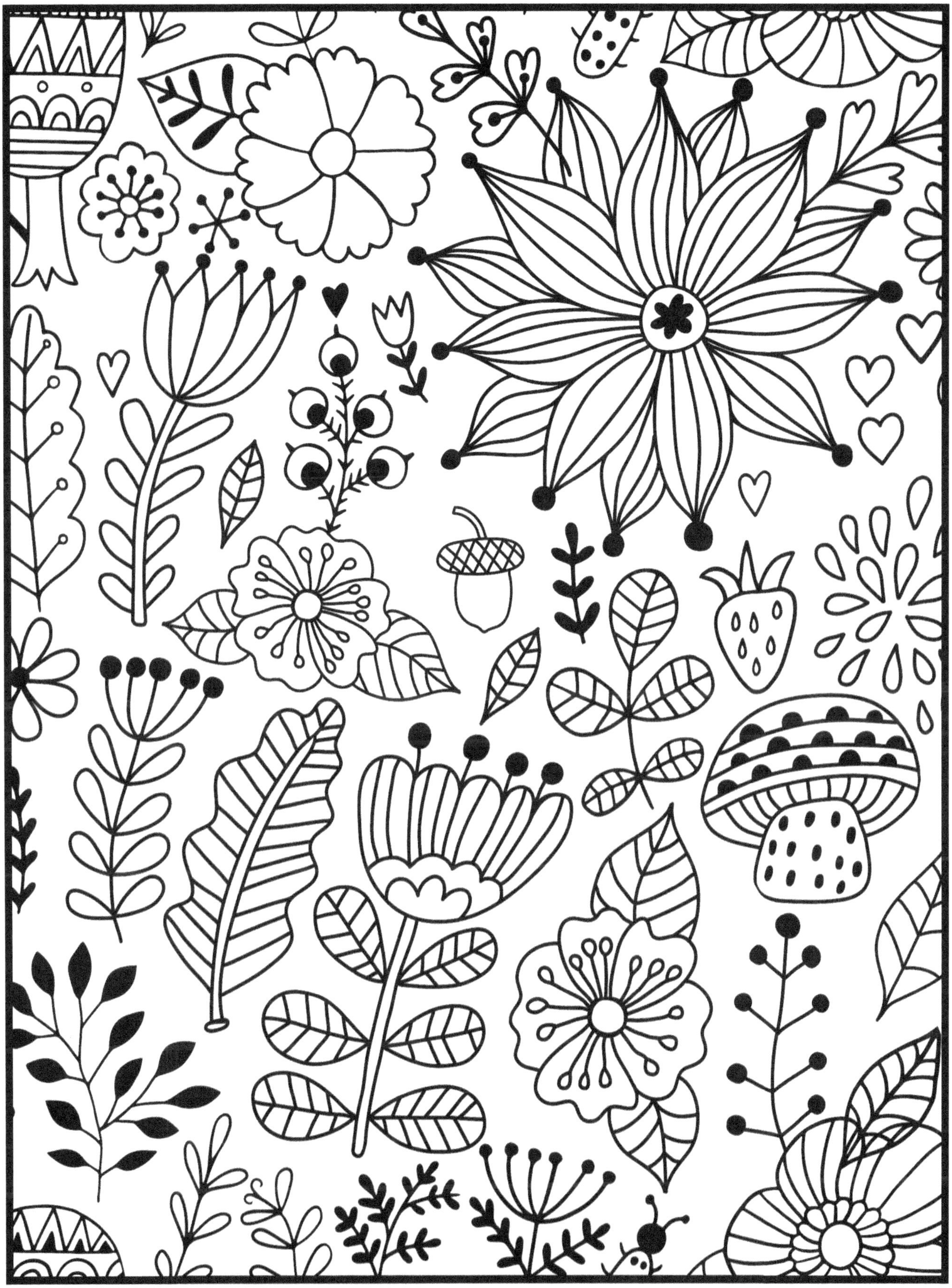

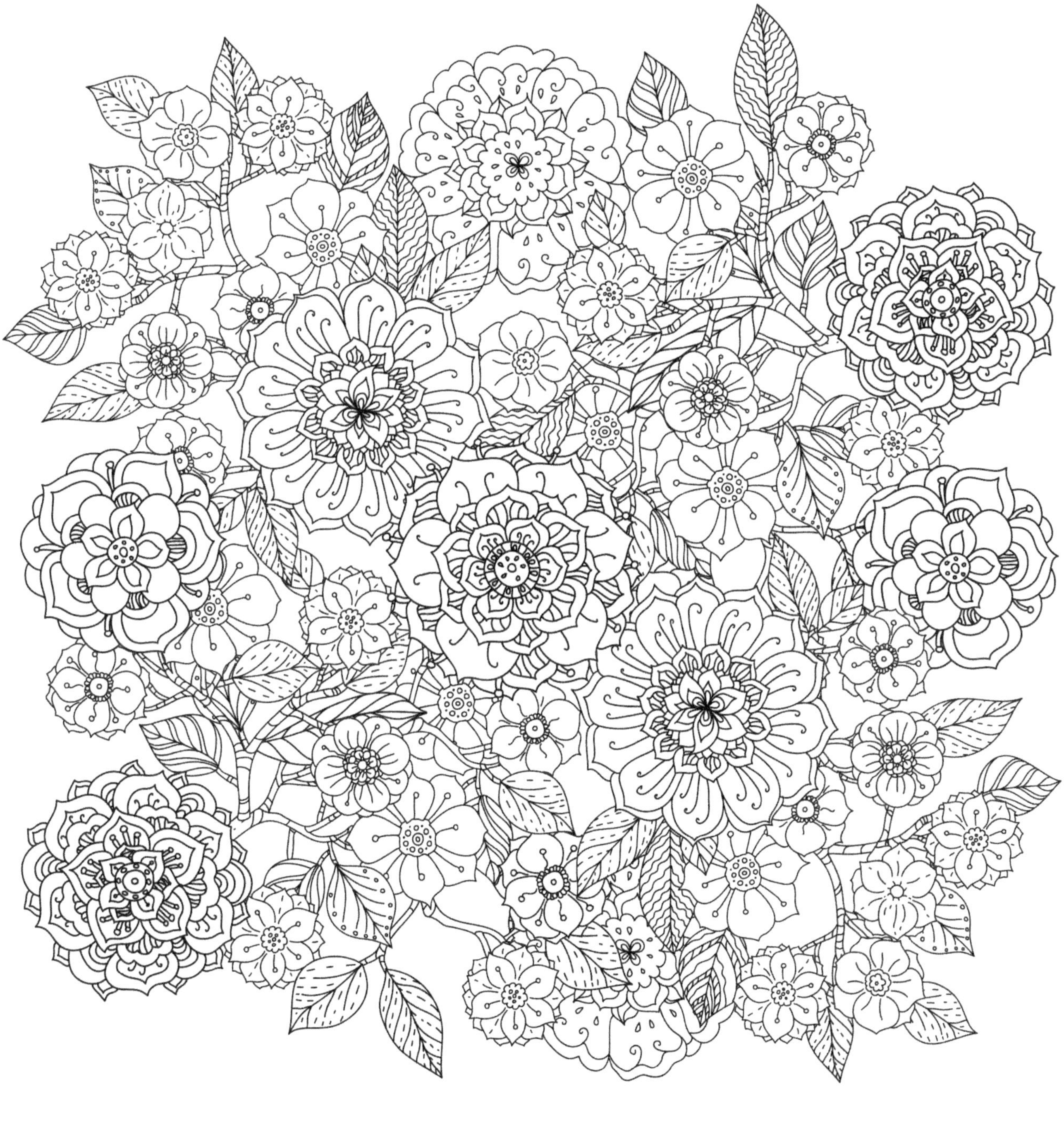

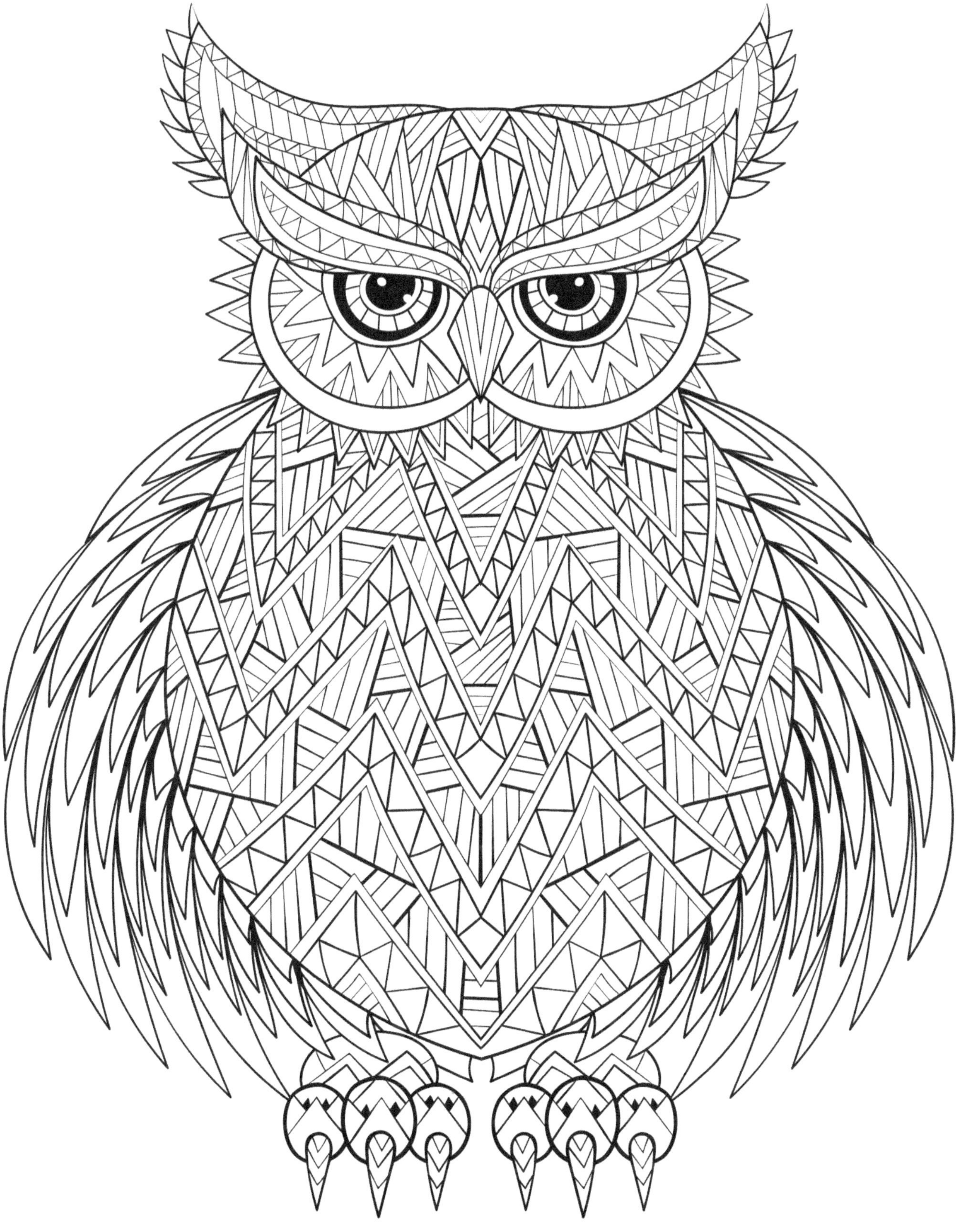

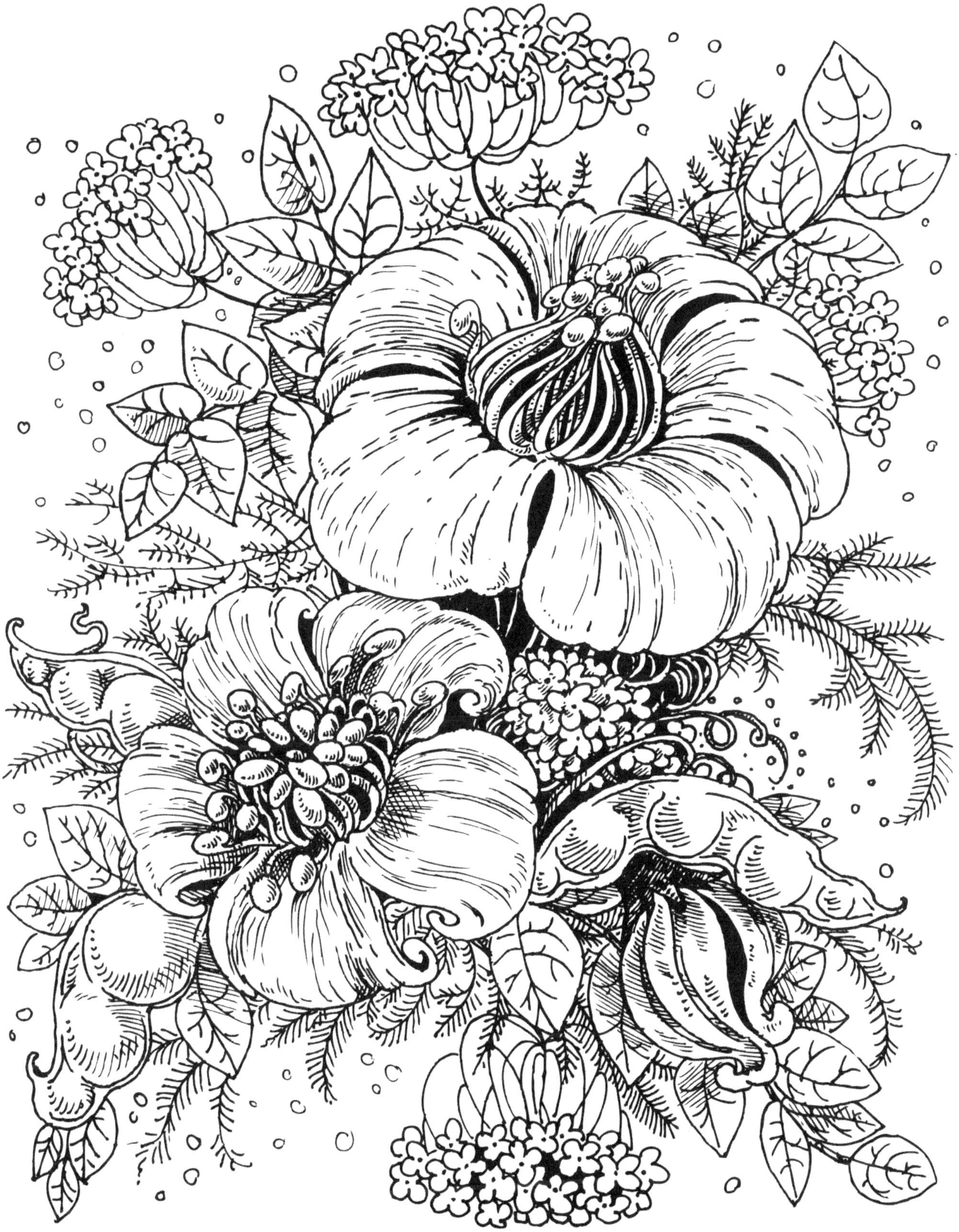

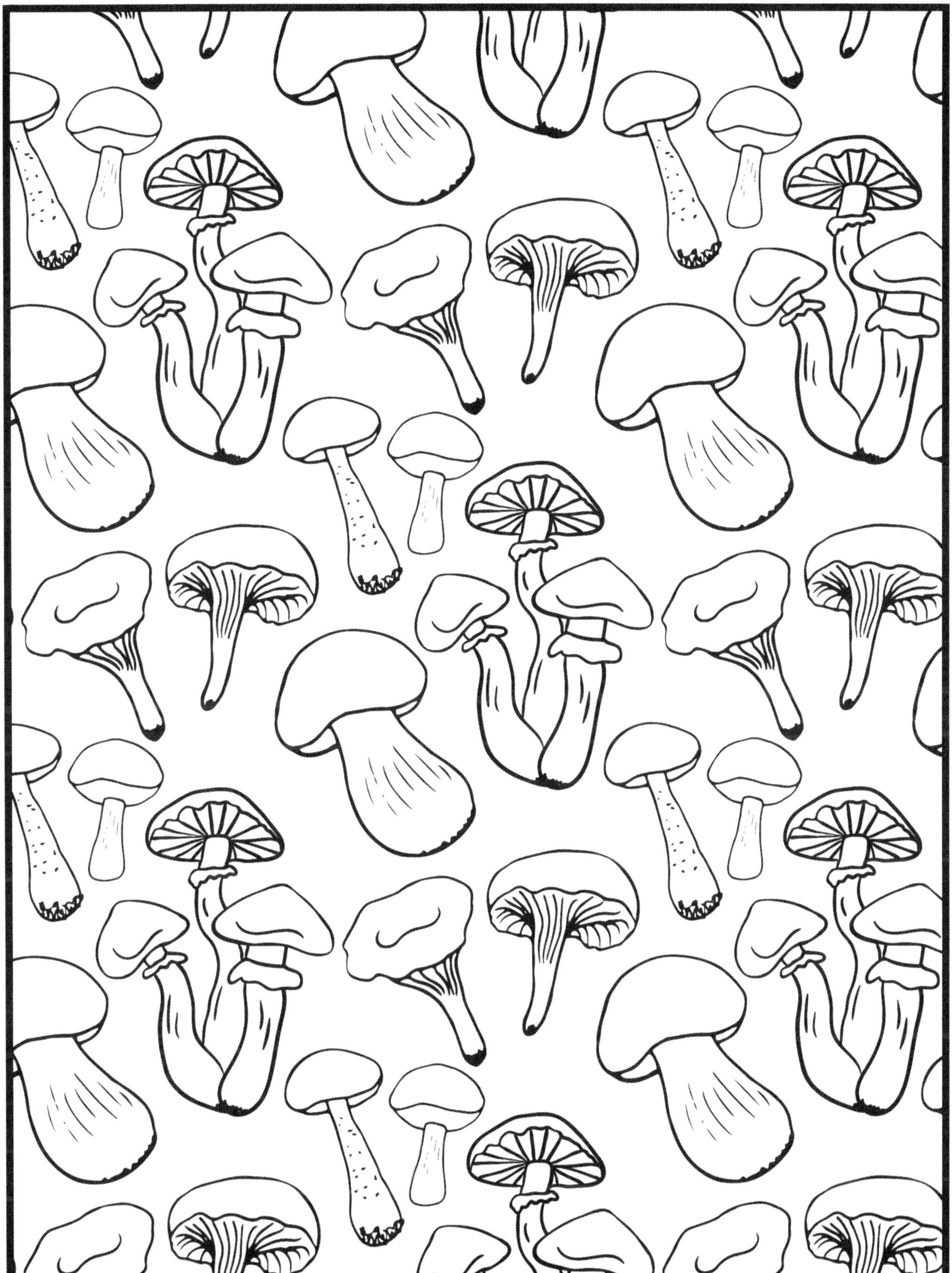

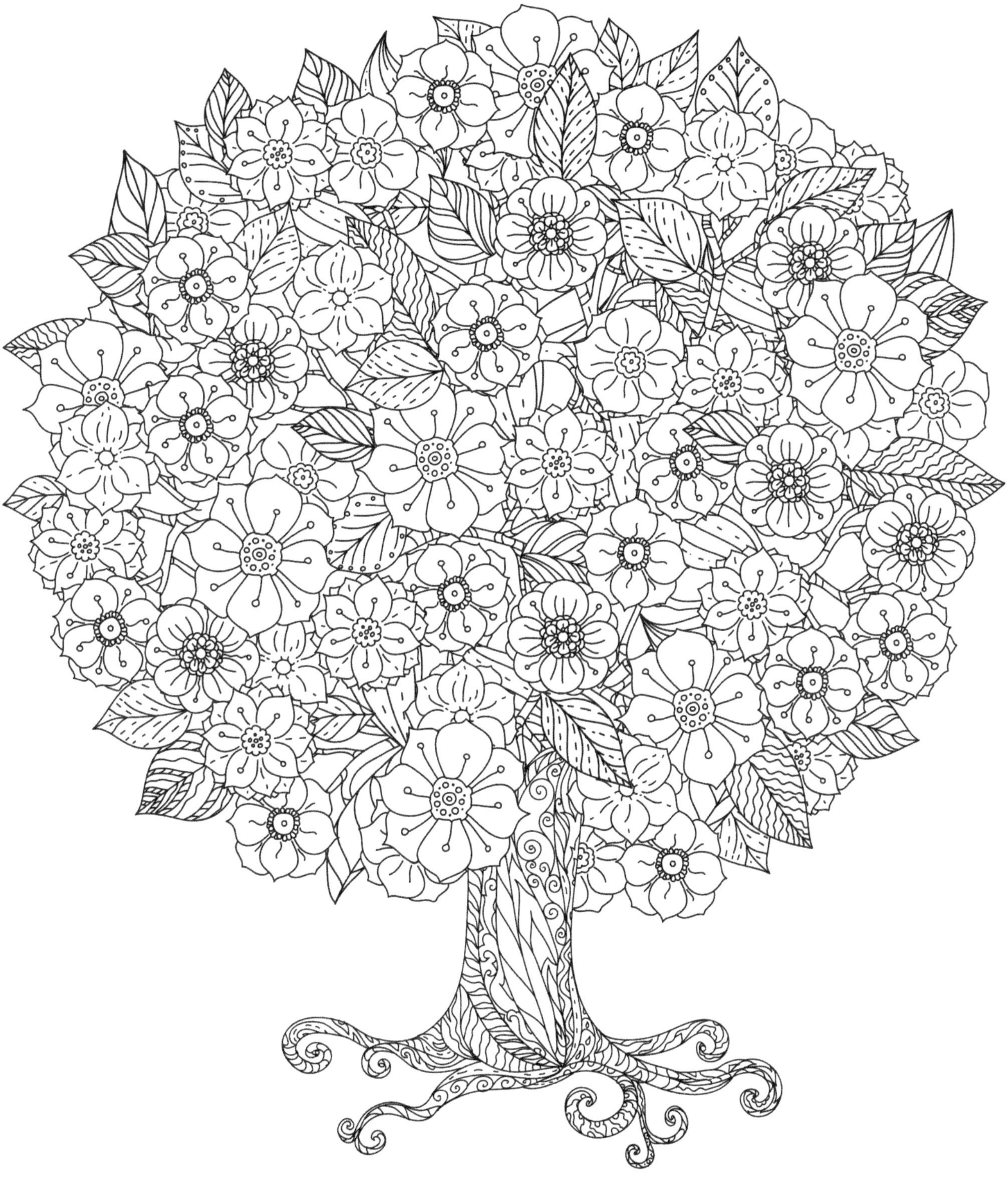

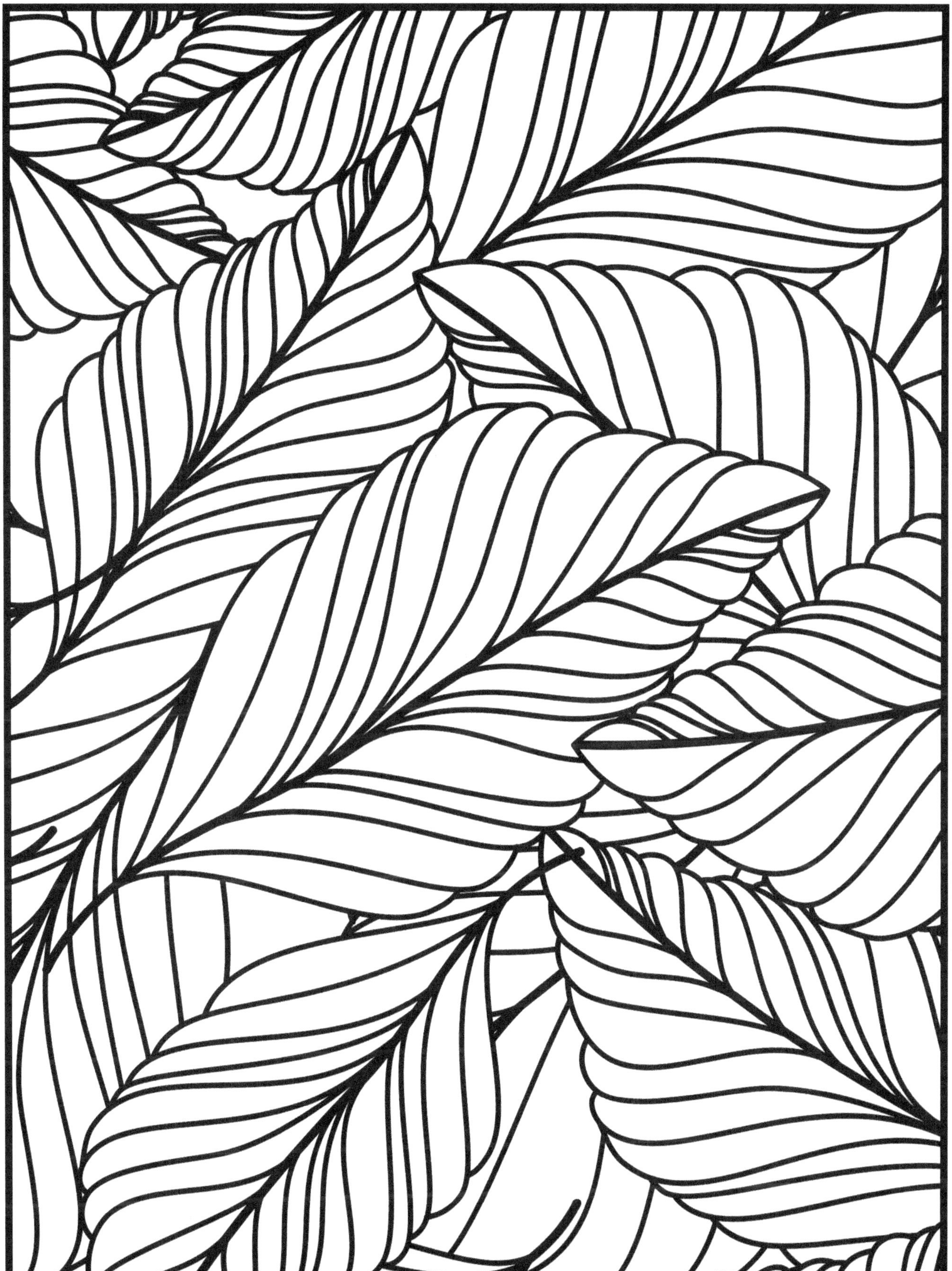

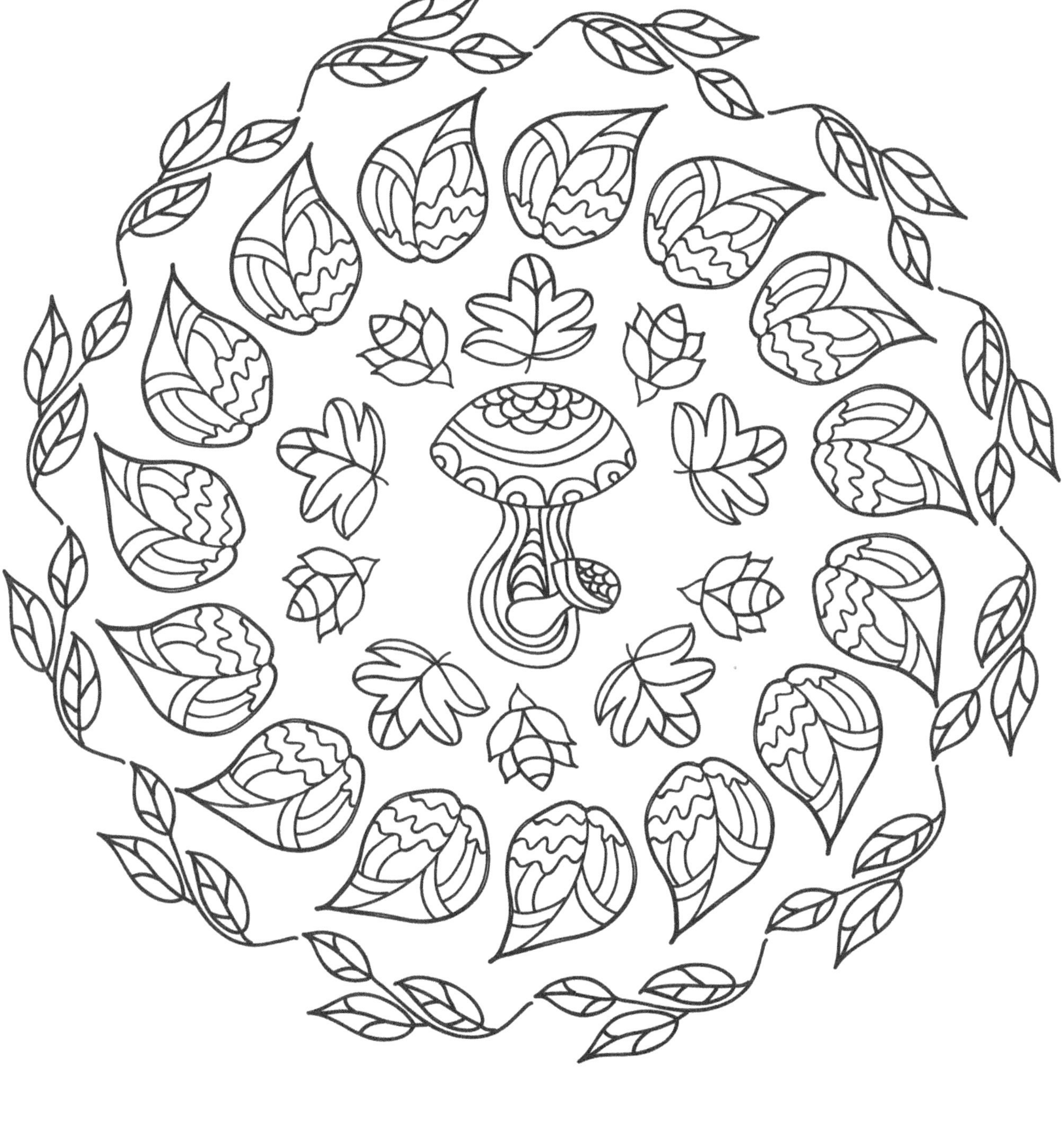

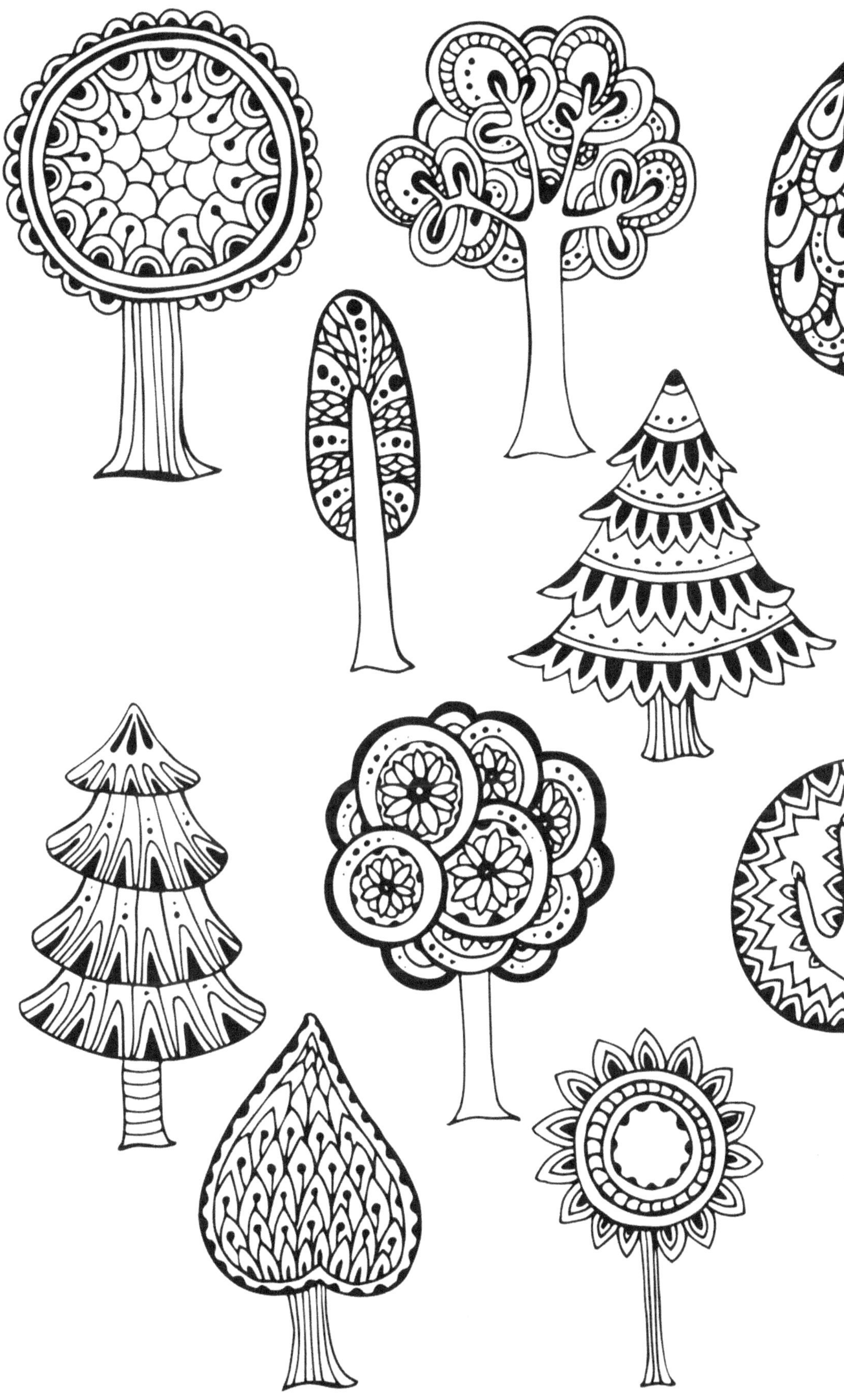

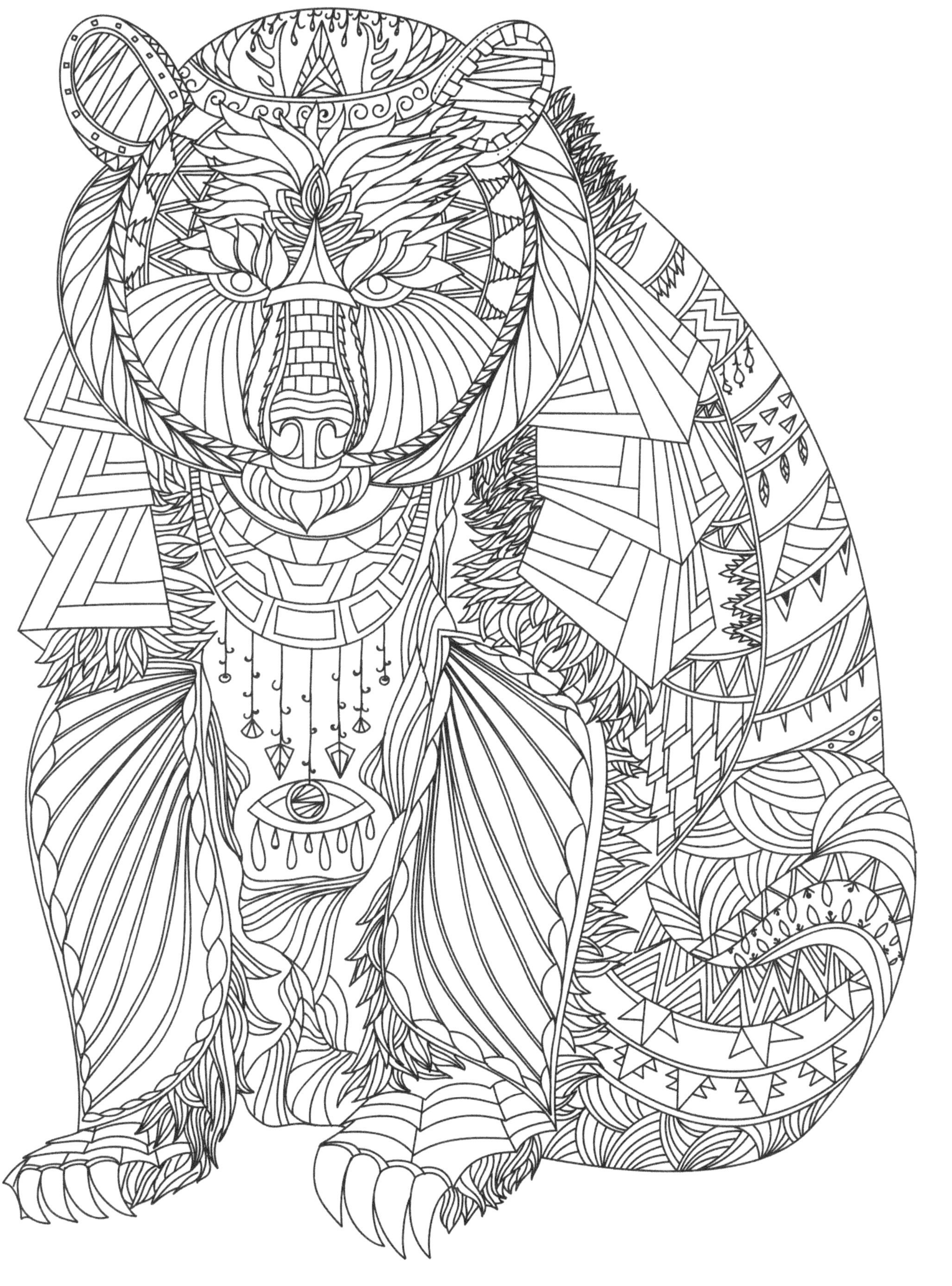

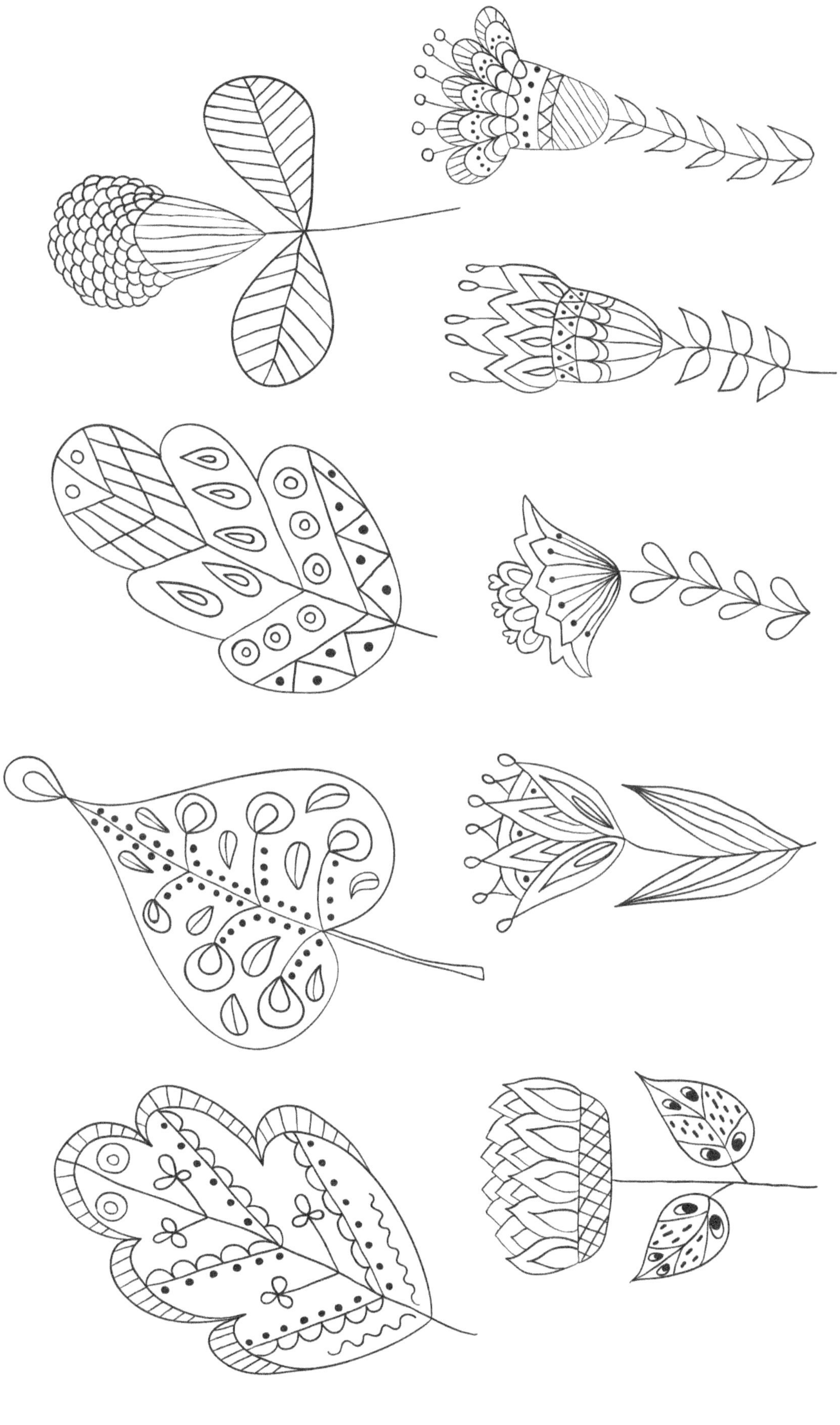

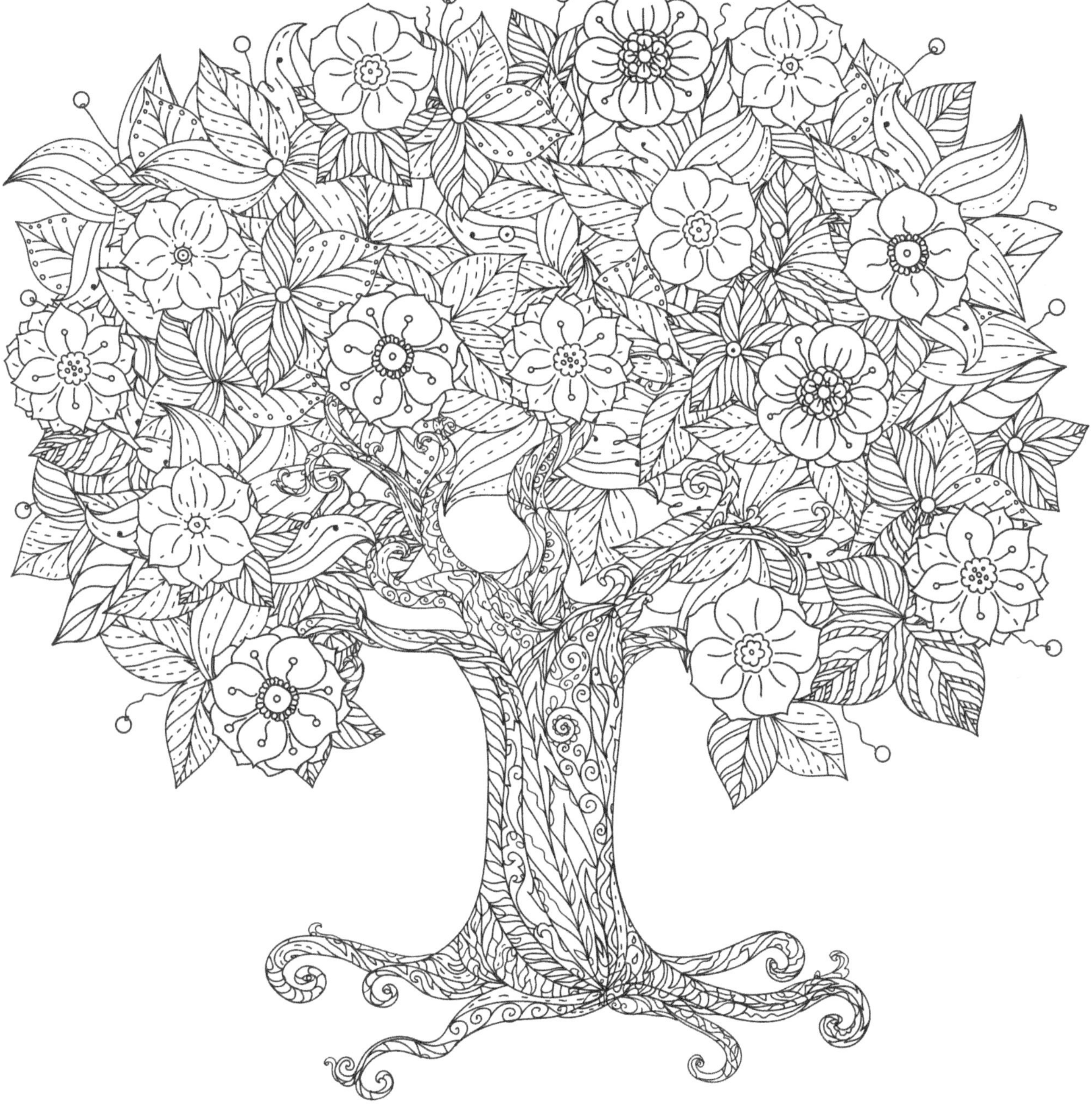

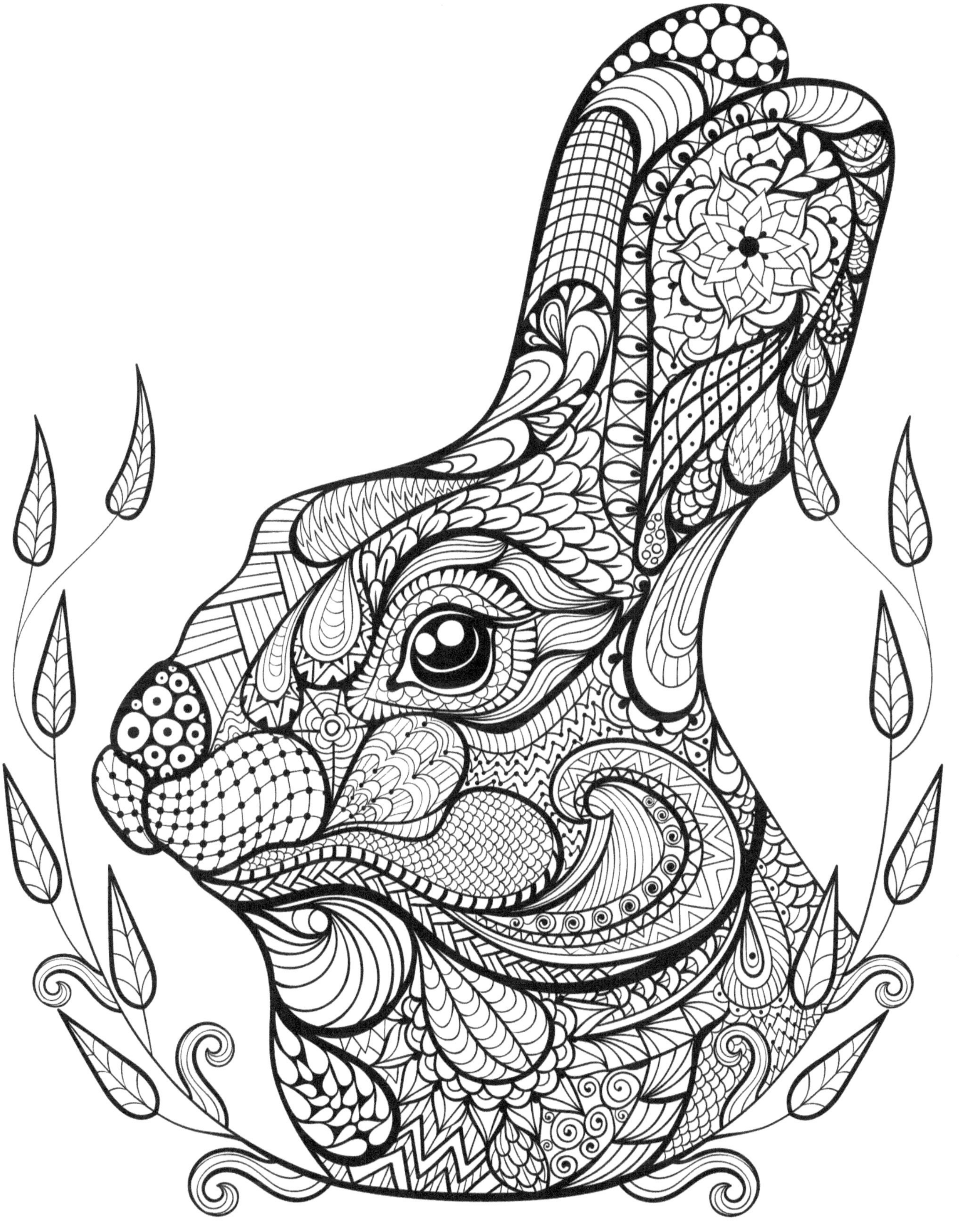

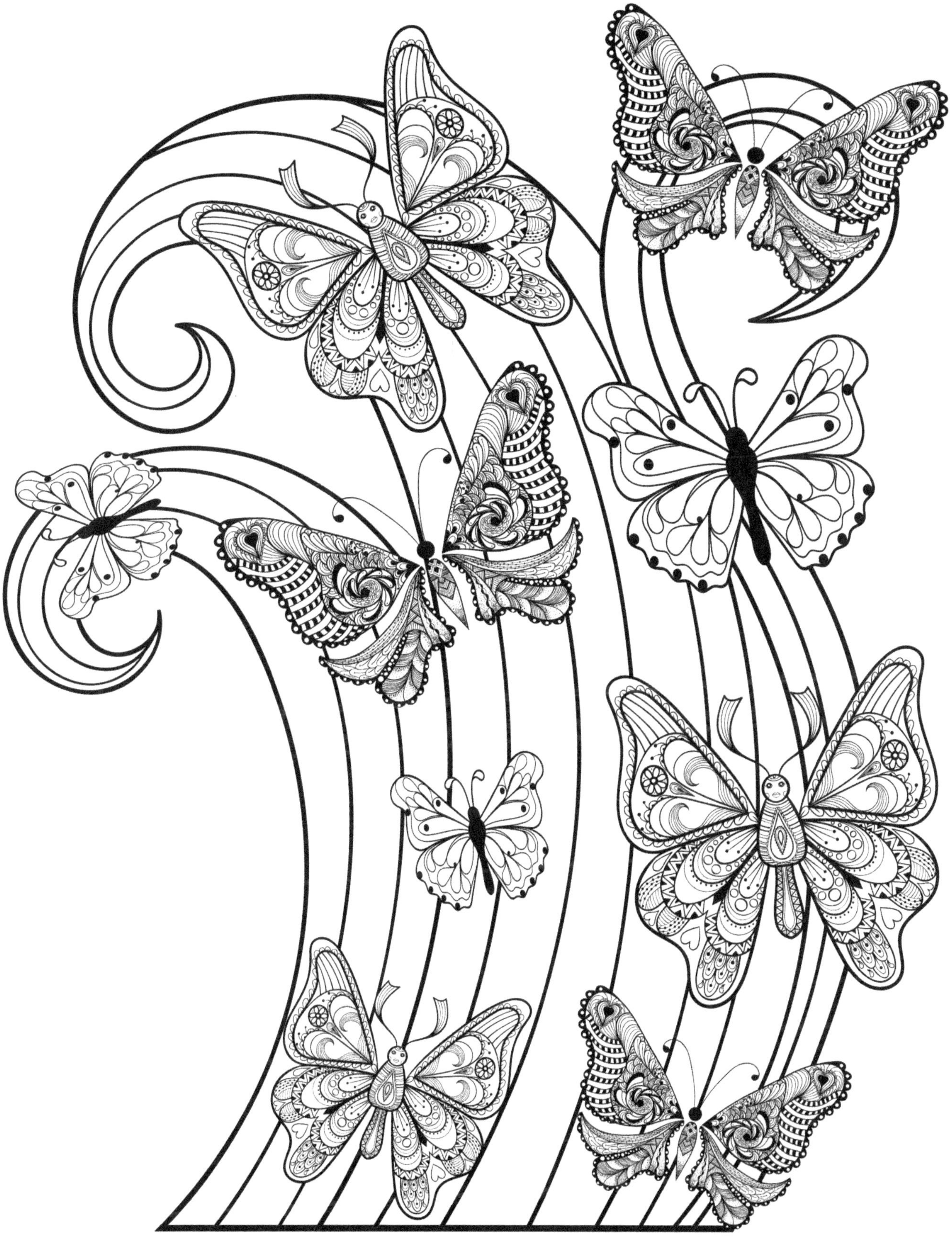

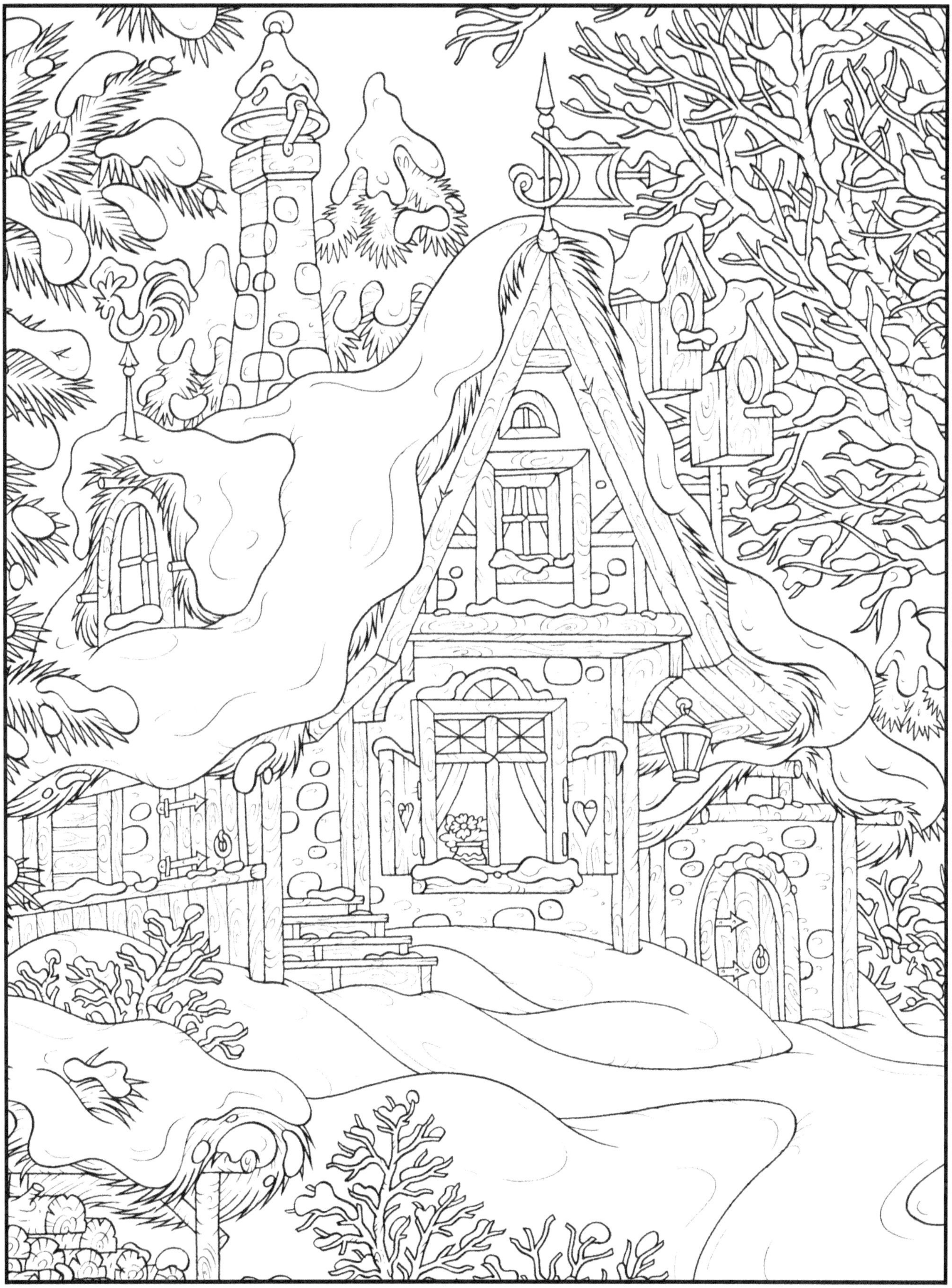

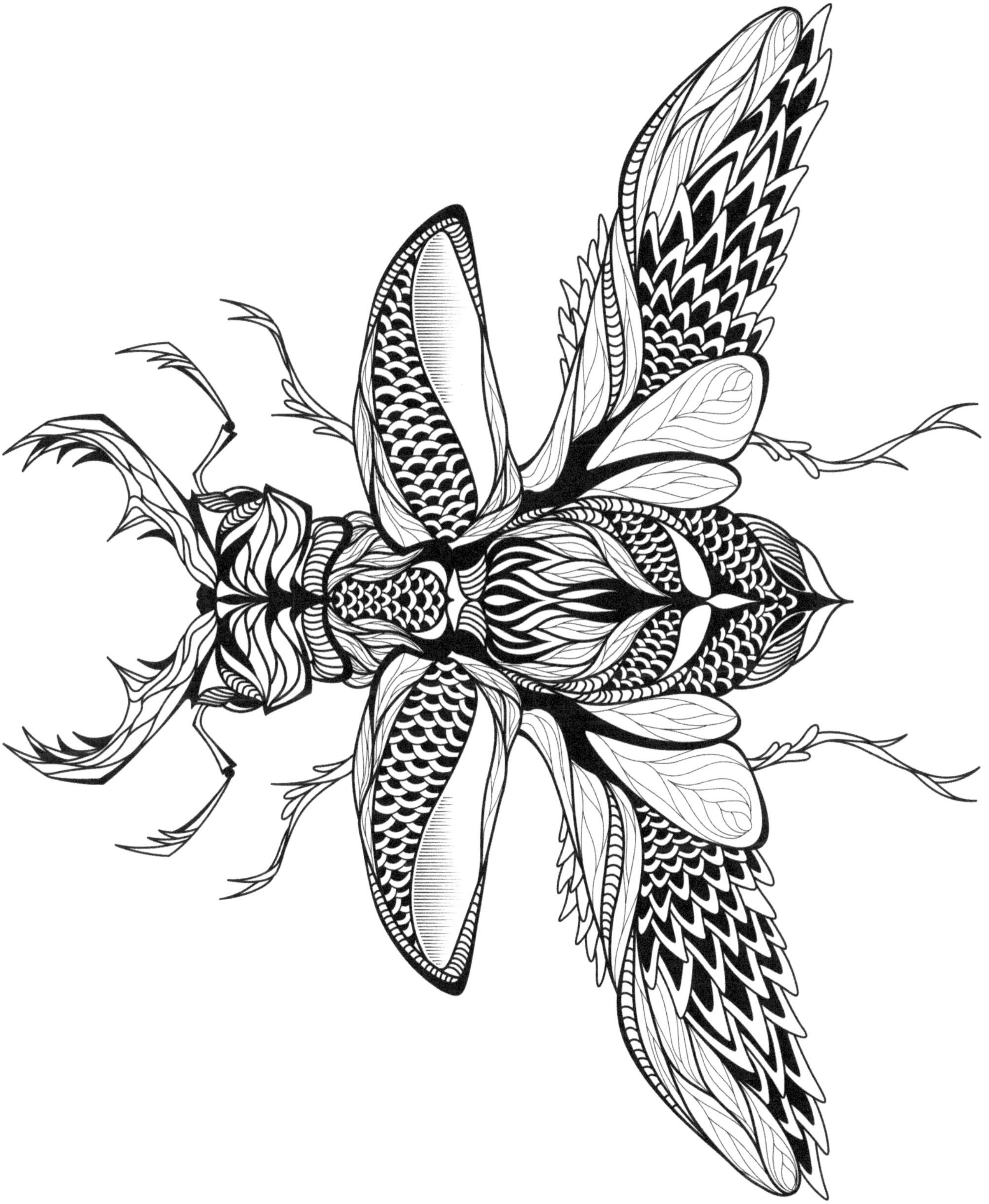

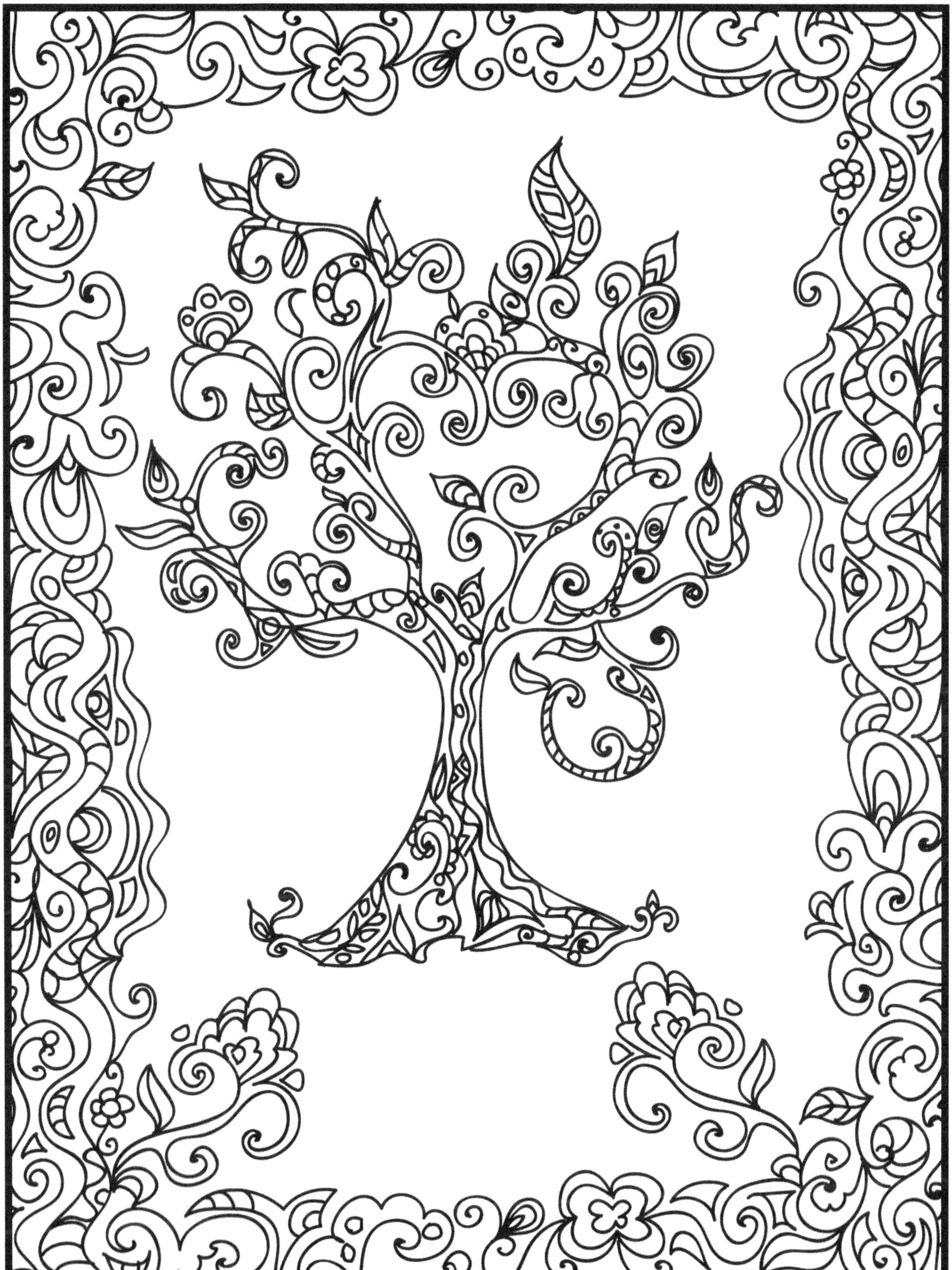

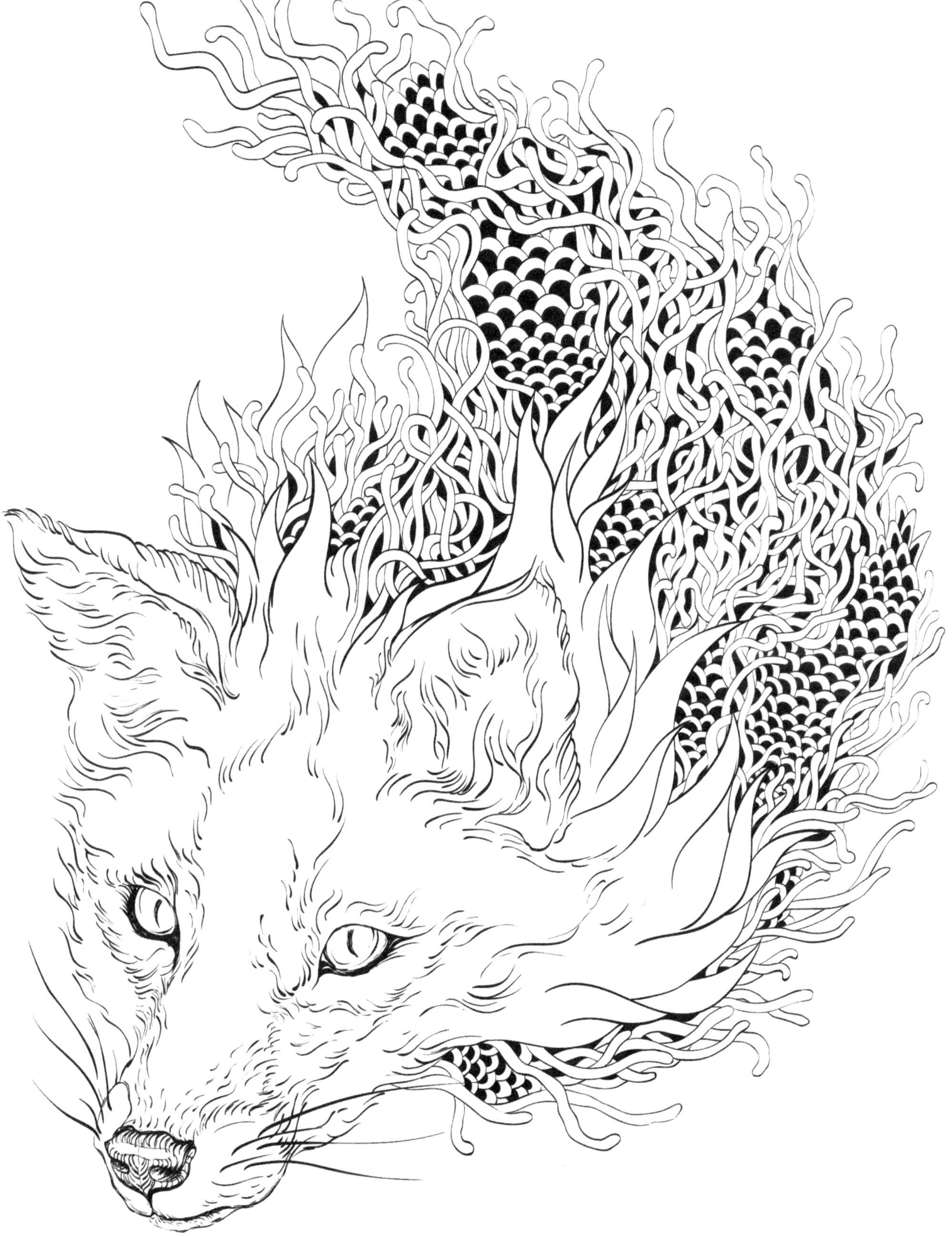

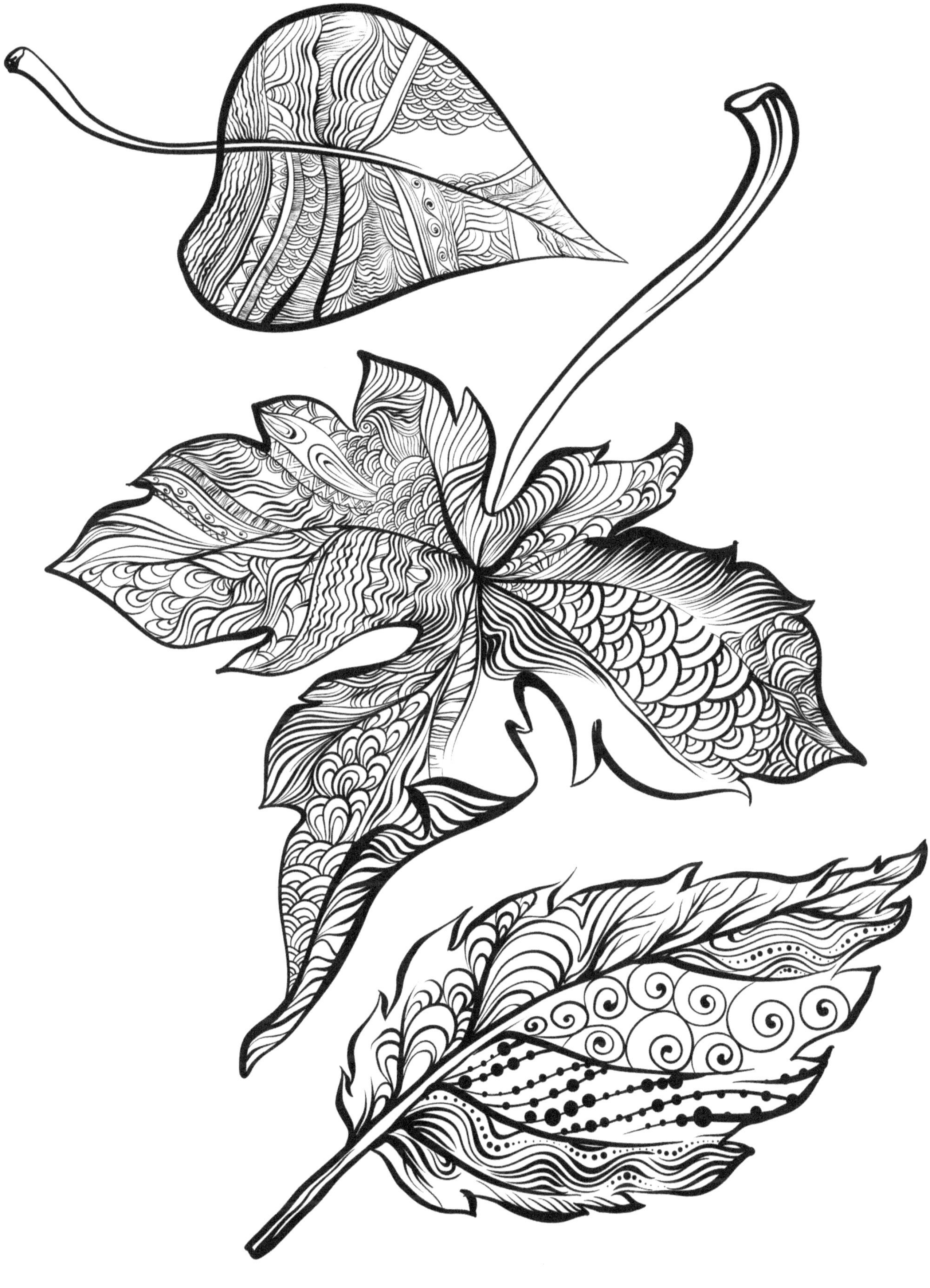

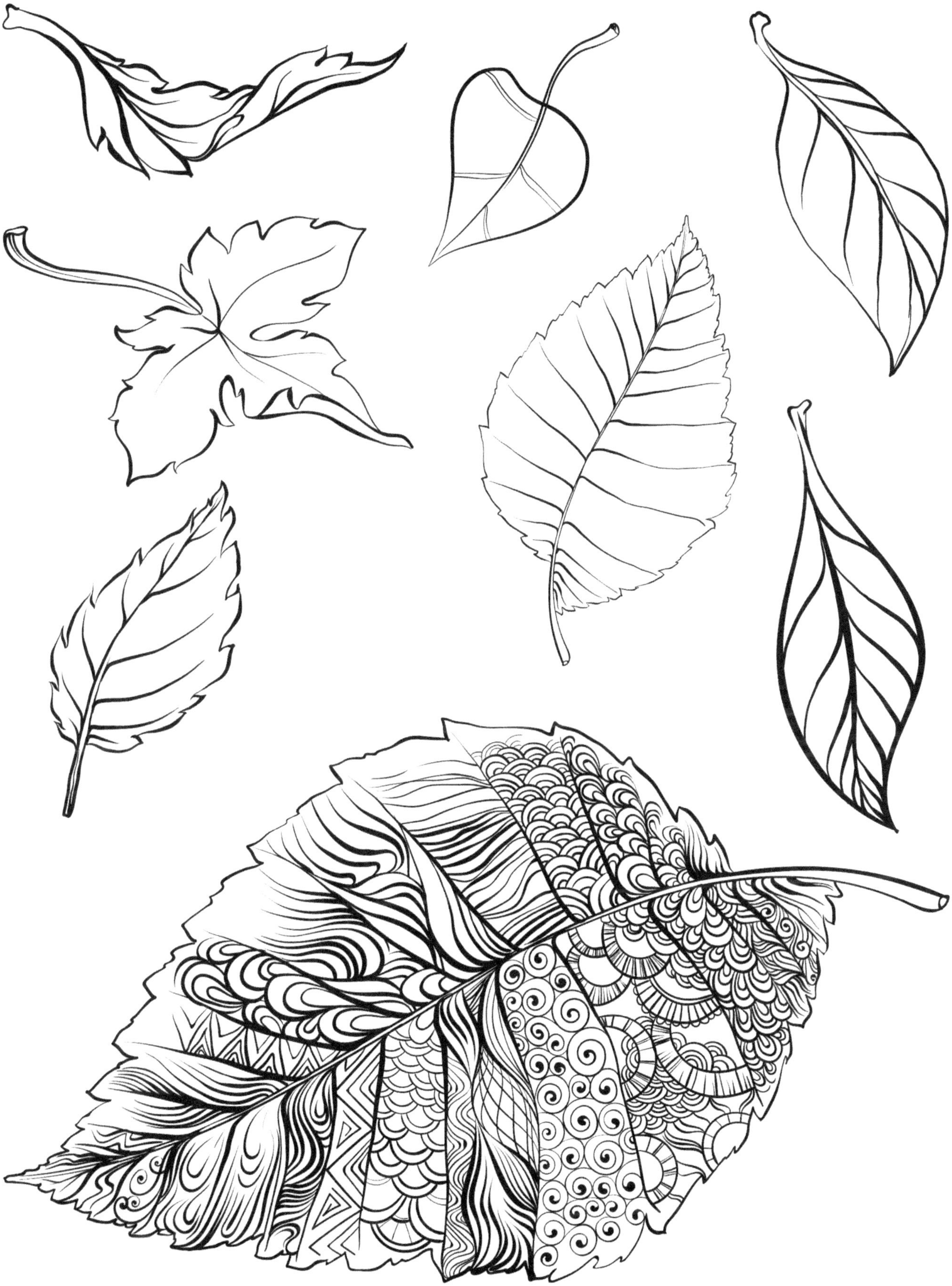

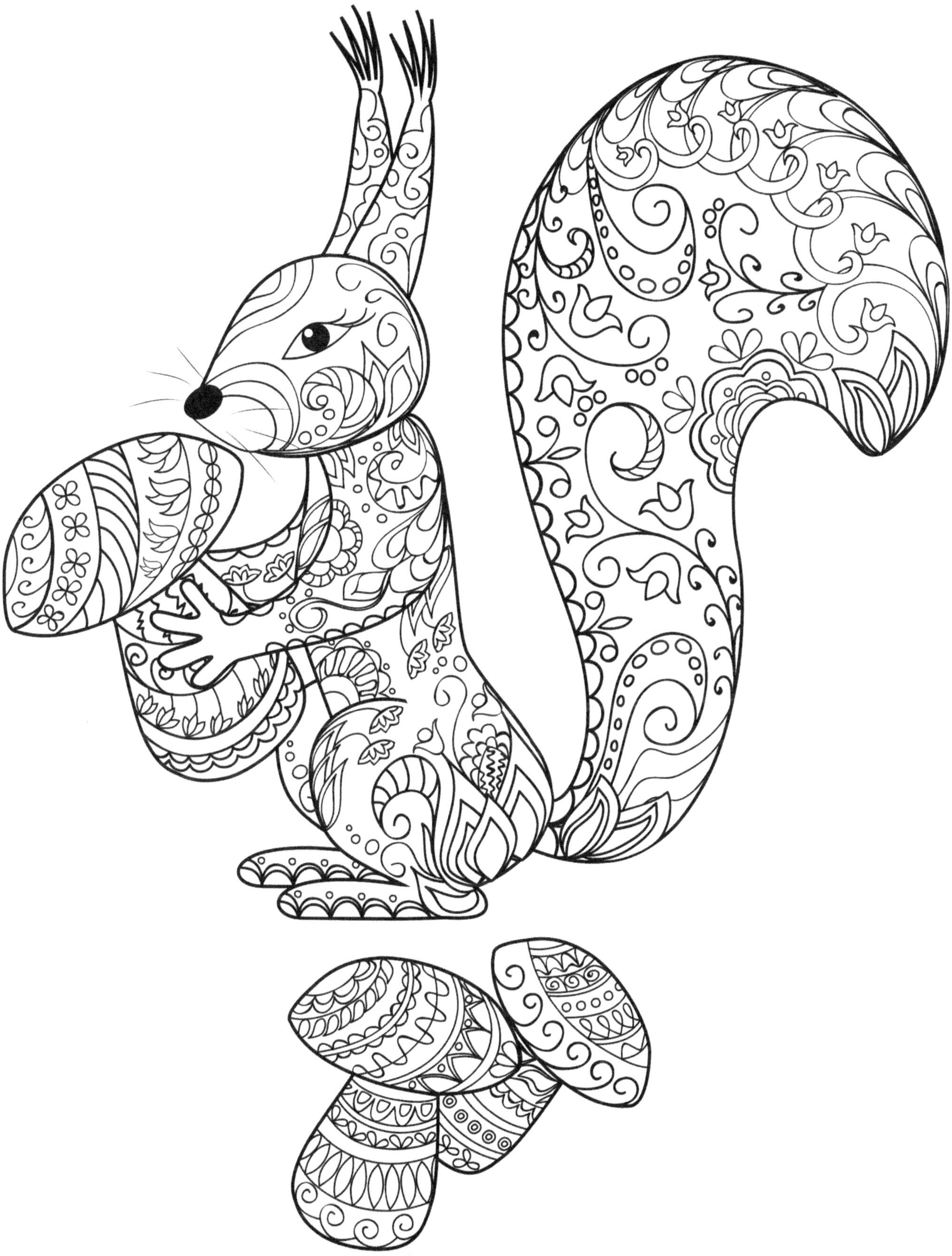

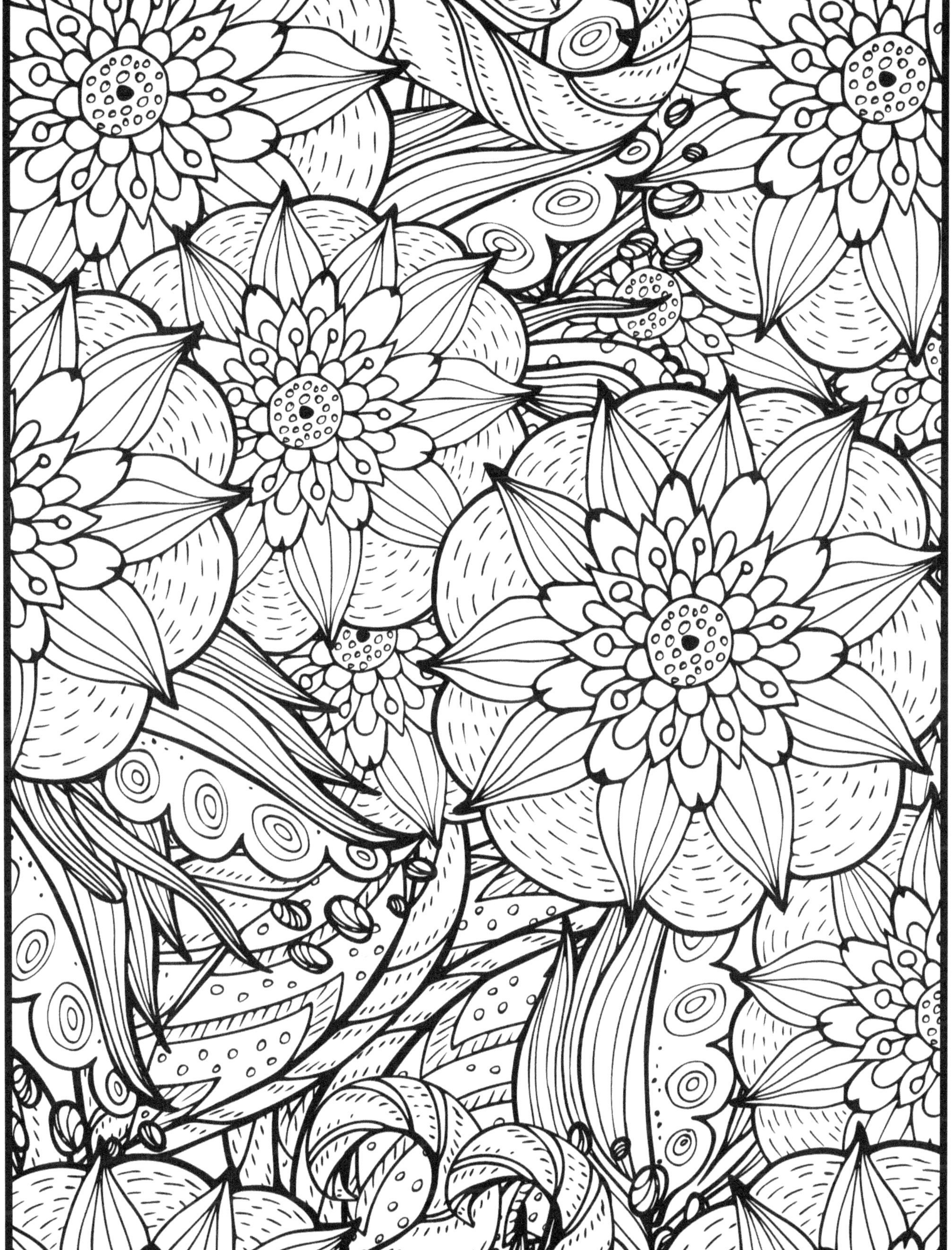

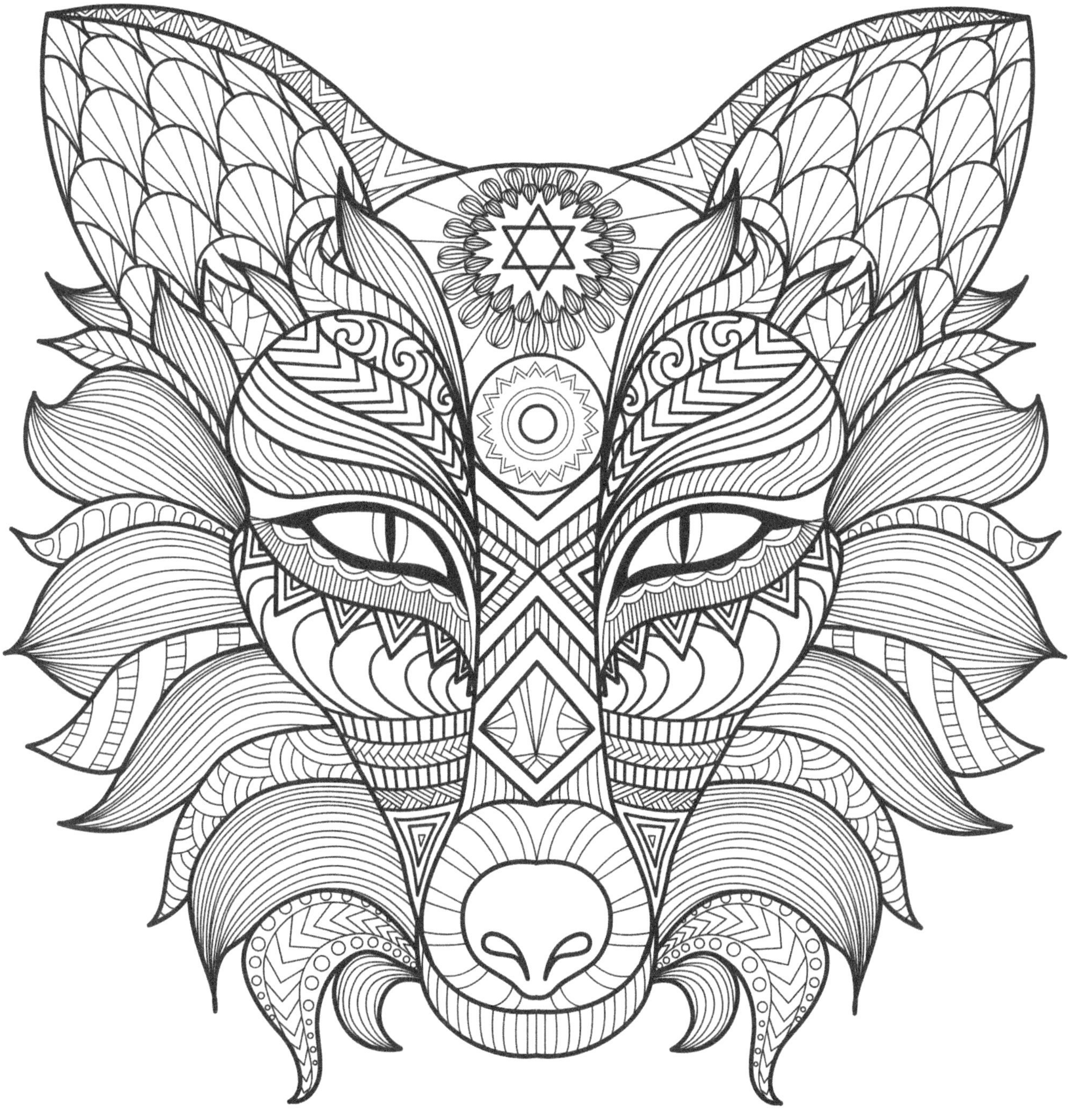

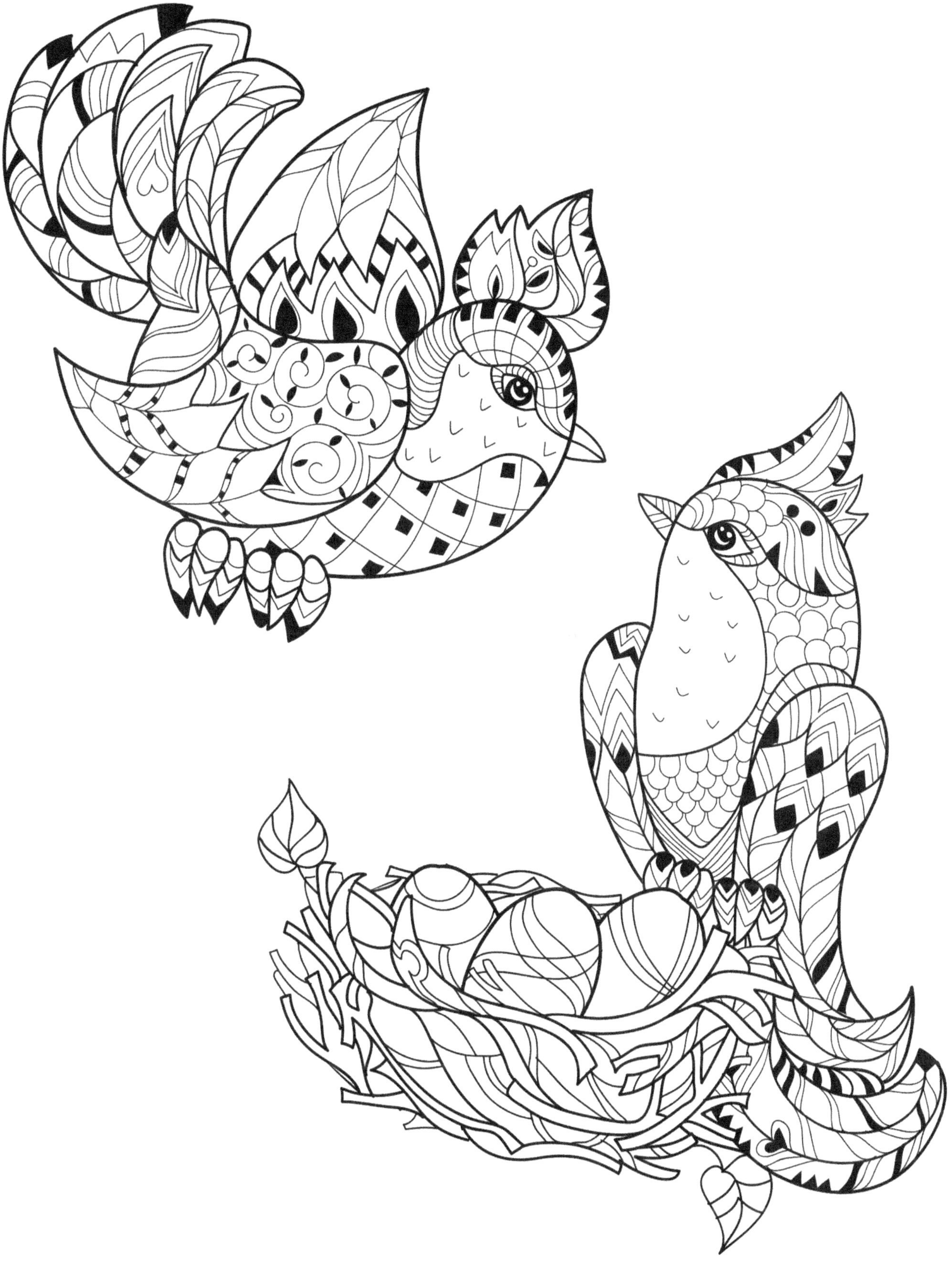

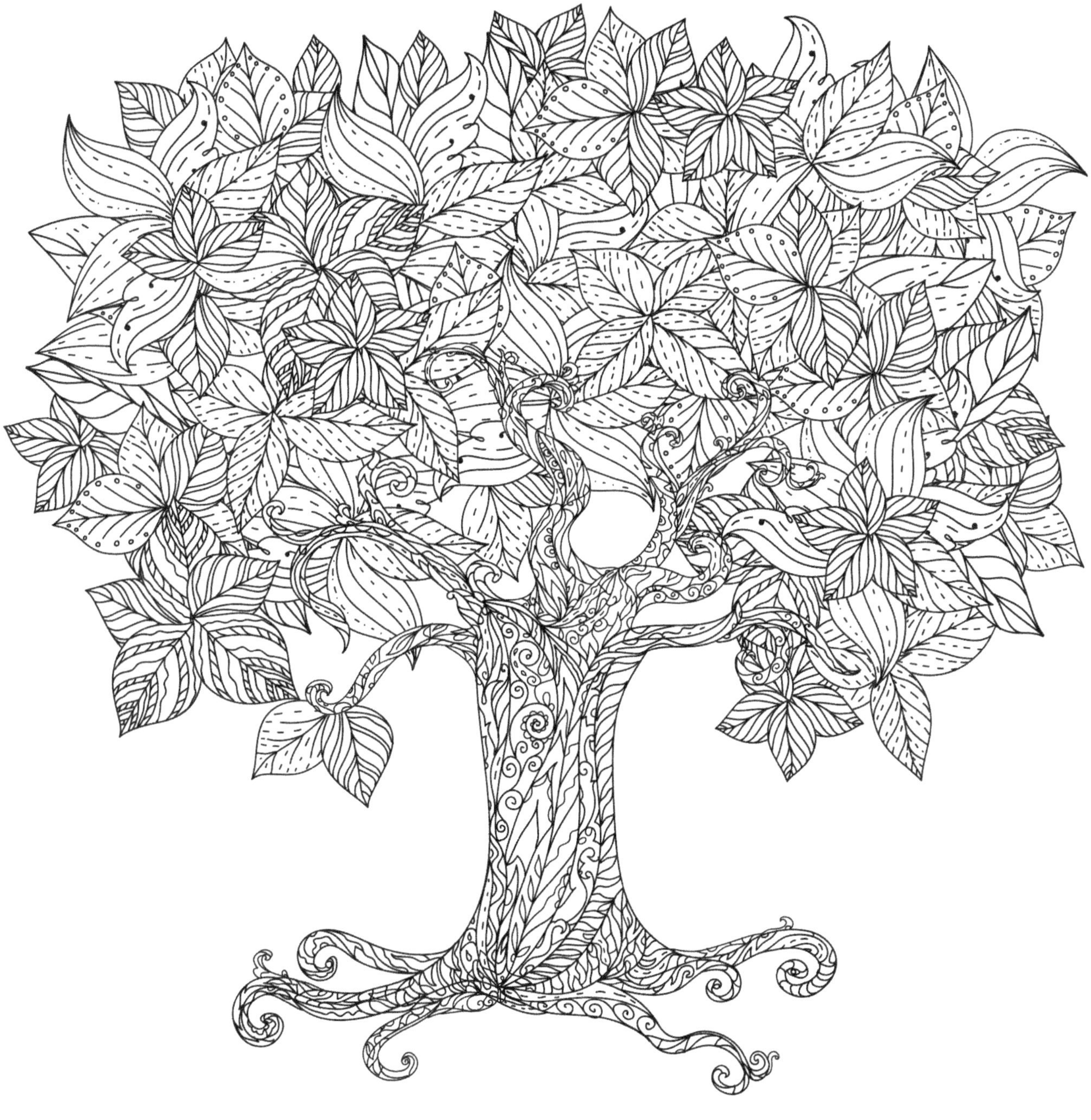